Skills Label ™

System to Manage and Track Skills

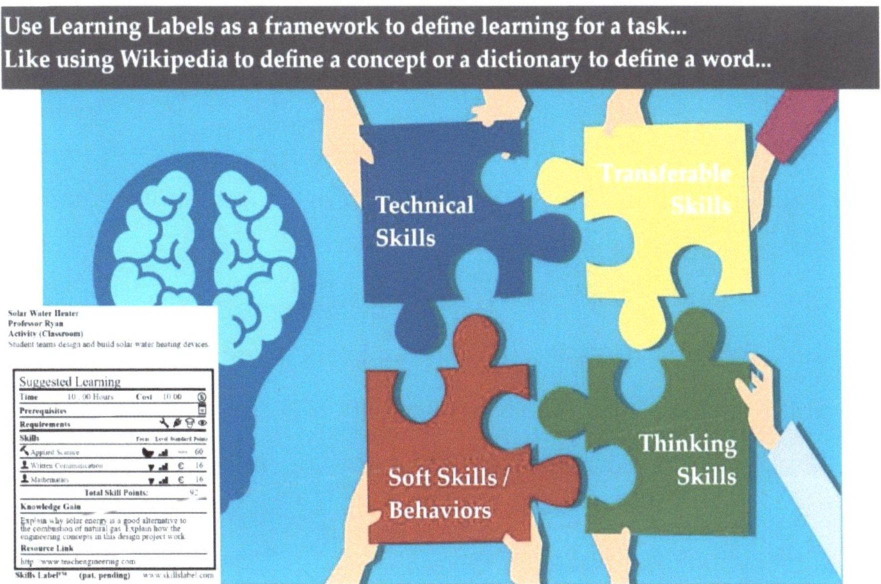

www.skillslabel.com | www.learninglabel.com | www.educationlabel.com

Map Learning in Skills. Map Jobs in Skills. Combine to Create Pathways.

By Ryan M. Frischmann

Contents

Introduction to Concept

Inspiration Behind Learning Labels

The inspiration for learning labels formulized as I was working on tasking in an application (Skills Based Approach). I wanted to reduce typing of information for each task, so with a learning label, one person creates the label and the information becomes available to all the users.

While working through the concept, I recognized the potential of a learning label – a standard representation of learning expectations as a display. I decided to move forward with intellectual property (IP) protection for the technology. Two prior art searches (2016 and 2017) did not reveal any close matches. A market analysis conducted by me and business students found competing services (at some level), but there is clearly a niche and differentiation for the learning label technology.

I hear the remark: "So these Skills Labels, they are like nutritional labels but for learning (education)". As I made clear the inspiration did not start with a nutritional label. Though later it had some influence. A nutritional label is a highly effective standard display, it: reads well – understandable to children to adults, informs, creates uniformity (measurements), and aids in making a basis of comparison. And these are also target attributes of learning labels.

Learning labels have significant other attributes:

- Optimized for a digital experience. They are interactive, scalable vector graphics that appear well on any device.
- Data can be interpolated over time. As learners consume resources, the data collected from the learning labels becomes available.
- Link to education / training standards. Most set of standards should work with learning labels.
- Learning gain calculated as a number. Each label has calculated Skill Points® to represent learning (the return part of a ROI).
- Interface to manage labels. Separate interfaces for learners and practitioners to manage labels.

Back to the nutritional label discussion. They are a very big deal. Most countries in the world have a 'nutritional facts label'. In the United States, the label was mandated for most food products under the provisions of the 1990 Nutrition Labeling and Education Act (NLEA), per the recommendations of the U.S. Food and Drug Administration (according to Wikipedia). Now, it is ubiquitous.

Children are taught to read the labels in school. Many of us make decisions on what we eat based on the information on the labels. Each of the past three administrations (Bush, Obama, and Trump) has in some way conducted policy based on these labels.

Maybe grandiose thinking, but I think there could be similar value with learning labels. There is so much happening in education and higher education, there needs to be some way to standardize a display of learning expectations; this does not mean to standardize the learning itself, but rather, how it is represented. How do we track learning across education, higher education, and career stages? How do we manage the distribution of various learning standards? How do we verify learning resources do what they are supposed to? Is it possible to put learners (including children) in control of deciding what learning experiences they want to do?

Thinking in skills and their methods and applications – the foundation of the labels – is the answer to many of these questions. I think being able to plug in any set of learning standards makes the labels powerful – districts, states, and countries can use their own standards. (One of the objectives of Common Core was to unify the education system, but in the intervening years states have been modifying their own versions of the standards.)

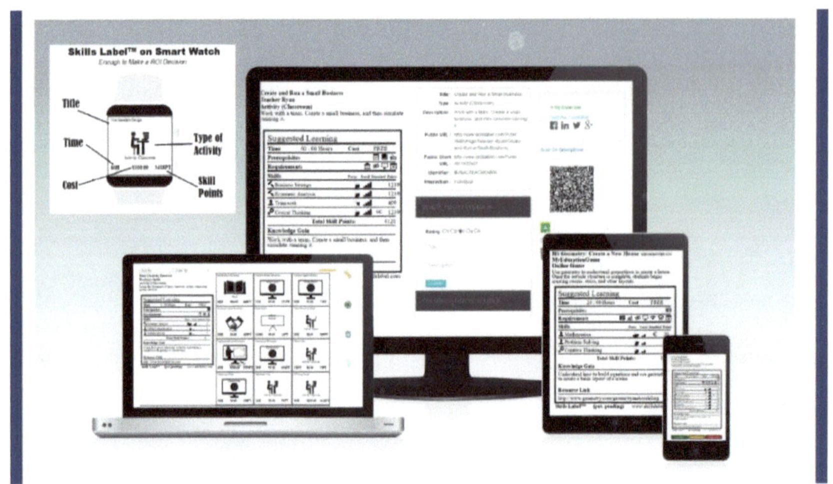

Learning Labels Solve Problems

Problem: There is no standardized process and display to attribute what has been learned from an educational resource. There is no way of comparing traditional learning types - books, classroom courses, with emerging learning types - online games and courses, IoT, etc. This becomes more apparent when comparing education, higher education, and professional learning resources. Some parts of the process are being applied, but there is nothing that collectively puts it together in a logical sequence and produces a result – a standardized learning display.

Education companies create learning resources and publish learning expectations; for example, Sim City builds a game to teach basic skills from Common Core. But there is not a standardized representation (like the proposed display) and there is nothing connecting learning expectations laterally across subjects and disciplines and vertically across learning stages.

Some web applications inform users how to acquire a credential and collect them over time. Mozilla has built one such platform with learning badges and creating a backpack to port them to other applications. However, this is limited as it focuses on validating one learning experience. Moreover, there is not a platform that suggests using all forms of credentials: certifications, learning badges, awards, etc. - like Skills Label.

With Skills Label, providers of educational resources have a step-by-step process to get their resource to an audience. The standardized display and credential can be accessed or found from an online search engine. The label might also be printed on educational resources found in a typical brick and mortar store.

Picture a student comparing skills labels (aka learning label) representing education resources and choosing one based on: cost or return on investment (ROI), how much time it takes to consume, learning preferences (like a type: book versus a game), or credential earned upon completion – all content shown clearly, concisely on the labels.

Solution: Skills Label™ is a patent pending process / method to create a standardized display, catalog, and database for what is learned from an education resource. All types of resources can be summarized using this process.

Skills Label™ differs from what currently exists. There is not a process for game designers, educational publishers, providers of online learning platforms, practitioners of traditional high school and college programs, and other producers of educational experiences to publish the learning expectations of their resources.

Skills Label™ is an improvement on what currently exists. It is a step-by-step process that navigates the producer or promoter of education resources in defining learning in a universal, standardized way.

Express Learning Expections for What and How You Learn

Macro Level Value

When you create an original concept, the focus is on how it solves a specific problem – on a micro level. As it gains momentum, the focus is on how it solves bigger problems – on a macro level. Over the past couple of years, I realized these learning labels have much more potential.

There are no borders. It is possible to express the learning expectations across districts, states, and countries. Substitute different languages to express the textual content if necessary. The icons are generally accepted across cultures. The definitions of skills are universally understood. Imagine distributing learning labels as a cross culture exchange of learning resources and their expectations.

There are no stages. The learning labels can be used in education, higher education, and training. Simply calibrate to the right skill competency. Plug in the relevant learning standards. Bridge these highly fragmented systems with a uniform representation of learning expectations.

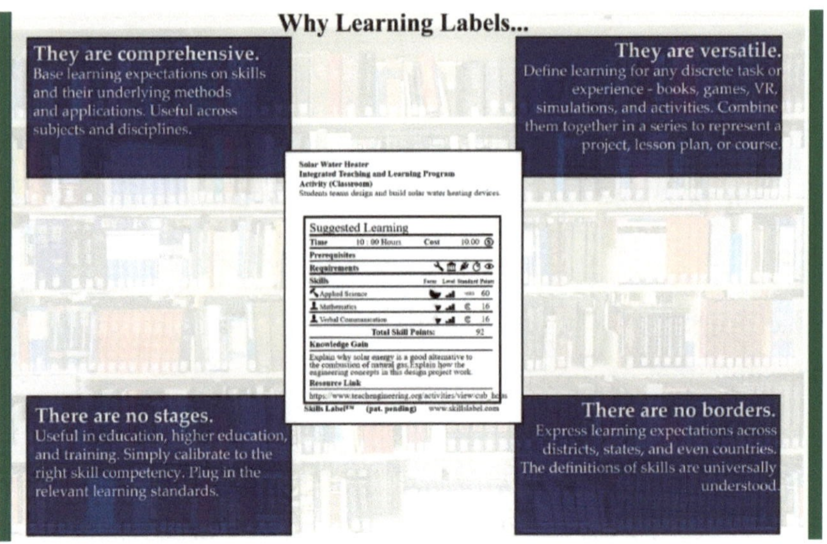

Figure 1 Macro Level Value in Learning Labels

They are comprehensive. Basing the learning expectations on skills and their underlying methods and applications, makes them useful across subjects and disciplines. Skills include foundational thinking (and their methods) and soft skills. Track the development of all learning in and out of the classroom.

They are versatile. It is possible to define learning for any discrete task or experience – books, games, VR, simulations, and activities. Combine them together in a series to represent a project, lesson plan, or course. There is new personalized grading functionality, so a learner automatically navigates through a series. Give learners the opportunity to choose how and what they are learning.

They are a basis for accountability. Institutions verify the learning expectations are accurate on the labels – like the FDA puts a stamp of approval on a nutritional label. In education, this might be like an accreditation process of a course. There is a verification process built into the learning labels technology.

How Long Does It Take to Learn a Skill?

Skills Culture is a growth mindset with a commitment to learn and apply skills properly. In trying to rally practitioners and learners around this mindset, important questions they ask are: How long does it take to learn a skill? How long is the commitment? These are good questions for someone who is expected to spend time and resources towards learning a skill.

Before getting into the details, it is worth defining the commitment - a central premise behind Skills Culture:

You commit to learning a skill each step of the way. This could be on a project or even a task level. You might learn a skill for your own personal needs or wants, what's needed for a project or job, or what's needed for a career. Regardless, you do not have to become a master of the skill. (If it is not required learning) pivot into learning other skills if you are unsuccessful or do not want to continue.

In this way, Skills Culture is a growth mindset. Someone learning a new skill is not encumbered with a preconception that they must become an expert, but rather remains in control of their learning experience. And that initial motivation is there. Most people believe they can learn a new skill if they put in the necessary time and effort.

The biggest factor in the time it takes to learn a skill is a desired level of expertise. Do you want to become a master? One benchmark is 10,000 hours to master a skill. This translates to about 9 years (consider 5 days a week, spending 4 hours a day).

Do you need it for a project? Do you want to explore a personal interest? One article says it can take 20 hours to learn a skill "to perform well enough for your own purposes." I think this 20-hour threshold for acquiring skills fits well with a Skills Culture. Josh Kaufman sums the sentiment well, "The idea of 'mastering' a skill when you're just getting started is counterproductive: it can be a significant barrier to exploring a new skill in the first place."

But basing a skill competency solely on time has problems. Someone with abilities or talents seemingly masters skills faster than someone without them and should also be able to complete more difficult tasks. Learning labels is ideal system to track the development of skills.

Skill Points® measure learning gains from completing tasks. They are calculated by a proprietary algorithm within the framework. Over a period, the sum of Skill Points® determines how far along a person is in developing a skill. If a person gets 1,000,000 points, then he or she has mastered the skill; but of course, this still takes a long time to accomplish.

Skill Points® is based on several factors, including time. So, someone with more ability or talent can skip to more challenging tasks and get credit for them – essentially moving up on the learning curve. Each learning label has all the information present to make a ROI decision to consume a resource. The investment values are time and cost. The return value is Skill Points®.

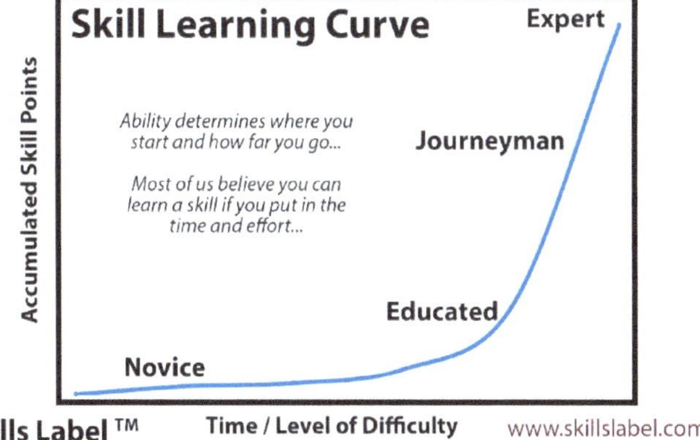

Skills Label A Step Towards Tracking Lifelong Learning

What replaces shelves of books you keep from education and higher education? The shelf where that dusty chemistry or finance book rests, which brings back memories of long hours of frustration (and that you never look at again). How do you keep track of learning for games you play online, activities in a classroom, or lessons outside of a classroom?

A collection of learning labels is an electronic catalog for all learning, essentially a summary of learning and index (and perhaps storage) to the resources themselves. And this not limited to books, but also includes games, activities, VR, experiences, and any task where learning takes place.

Skills / Learning Labels is a step towards tracking lifelong learning. It is a patent pending utility which involves creating a label, assigning learning expectations / outcomes, verifying the accuracy of the assignments (optional), and designating a credential. Let's breakdown each step:

- A label itself is a standardized display for any discrete task or experience.

- On the label (and landing page), there is a link to the resource itself.
- Learning expectations are largely expressed as a 'Skill Line Item', which is based on skills, their underlying methods and measurements. It is also possible to anchor them to standards.
- There is a verification process based on a peer review. Later, this process might be supported with AI or machine learning.
- Upon successful completion (of the task or experience), the learner has access to a credential. This might be a badge, award, or certification.

Either through an LMS system (like Google Classroom), a skills tracking system (like Skills-Based Approach), or the Skills Label user interface, users can easily find, access, and collect these labels over time. There a few advantages:

- LMS systems in K-12 and Higher Education is fragmented, so students are using varying systems. Skills Label is a standardized representation.

- A significant amount of learning takes place outside of the classroom, not in the jurisdiction of school assignments. Students / professionals should get credit for this learning.
- There is no way to compare traditional and emerging learning technologies. Many of the new applications– online games, VR experience, etc. – do not explicitly state learning objectives.
- Being largely based on skills and methods, the labels work laterally across subjects and disciplines and vertically across education and career stages. The labels are meant to have continuity, so are not only useful in depicting learning from a task but also bridging past, present, and future learning.
- Sum Skill Points® through time.
- A platform to "stack credentials".

The whole matter of 'tracking' is unobtrusive, controllable by the user, and (with validated labels) has significance. It is unobtrusive - meaning a user simply finds the label, consumes the resources, and stores the label in a collection. (If the student is at a store, simply scan a QR code to access the label.)

A series of labels, representing completed tasks, assignments, and experiences is a convincing way to track lifelong learning. Later, the data collected from a label and interpolated over time provides valuable insights regarding personal learning. This has advantages:

- Measuring and using skill competencies creates agile workers. For any career change, a worker accesses a current learning path (data from a collection of labels), finds gaps in skills, and then fills them. (Faster and more efficient than going back to get a degree.)
- Students / professionals have access to the learning resources that impacted them the most.
- Shareable with a counselor, teacher, mentor or supervisor as a personalized learning track.

Keep a Record of Learning

A key aspect of competency or skills-based learning is an assessment – evaluation or estimation of a person's ability. It is intriguing to play a game, complete a project, or take a test and through an assessment get an accurate portrayal of a competency – like taking the SAT, GMAT, or LCAT, which produces a score of a capability in a field of study. But these standardized tests have a similar shortcoming in that they do not consider the context behind the knowledge –experiences.

For this reason and others, there is value in tracking the successful completion of learning tasks – a record of learning. An assessment might be included within or after a task or series of tasks.

To illustrate the relationship between a task and assessment, consider this example. The task is to read a chapter in a book and answer the required questions. A teacher is pleased if everyone has completed the task, he or she has something to work with in the lecture. An assessment takes a next step and evaluates how he or she answered the questions to determine a grade and perhaps what task to do next.

A few reasons why there is value in tracking the completion of tasks, a record of learning:

- Provide context based on experiences. Get a basic understanding of what learning has taken place and how.
- Develop a learning plan. Move through a series of tasks based on performance.
- Track methods and applications. Understand how skills are applied.
- Get credit for non-required learning. There are many ways of learning outside of the classroom.

- Include cross disciplinary knowledge. Tasks often involve learning skills in different areas.

Learning labels is an ideal platform to track learning for the following reasons:

- Quantifies learning with Skill Points®.
- Creates a basis (language) to interpret learning over time – skills, their underlying methods and applications, and education and training standards.
- Connects into a series (learning plan, project, or course) based on performance.
- Establishes a basis of comparison.
- References all skills.

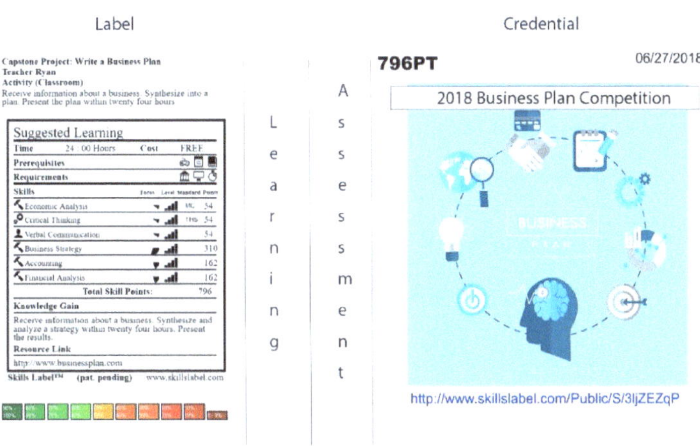

Skills Label™ Process: Label, Assessment, and Badge

Figure 2 A Record of Learning

Tracking Skills and Their Underlying Methods and Applications

I have been working on tracking skills in applications since 2011 and convinced we need to get a level deeper by tracking the imparting of methods (represented as a framework) and applications (technology or specific use) in applying skills. Much of this is done implicitly (as teacher's and experts know the methods they are teaching), but let's make it explicit by tracking what methods students and young professionals are learning.

Four big reasons why:

1. **Basis to understand a competency.** There is not much value in saying: "I have been applying critical thinking for ten years." But if you can say: "I induce, deduce, verify and summarize when I solve a problem. Give me one and I will show you." Then, you prove this. There is context.
2. **Move forward in learning a skill.** Some skills, like ones related to communication, you learn throughout your life. The methods you apply might gradually become more sophisticated.
3. **Signal chosen methods and applications.** Some technical skills are extremely broad and do not mean much on their

own. For example, someone applies the skill of 'Economic Analysis' in many ways. Or a web designer chooses a scripting language ASP .Net, Java, or PHP.

4. **Situational application of skill.** Different situations require different applications of skill.

Tracking the Development of Skills and Their Underlying Methods and Applications

Learner Centric Application (v 2.0)

There is so much focus on institution centric applications, such as learning management systems ("LMS"), credentialing applications, and systems for education publishers.

Learning institutions need to control and verify how learning objectives are achieved. They craft learning paths and provide credentials with their reputation on the line, so have a steadfast commitment for quality control of their programs. So, the questions are: Is it possible to put learners in the 'driver seat' of their learning? Can we design applications focused on the decision-making of a learner?

There is some proposed value in this:

1. **Navigation**. Access resources beyond the confines of an institution's applications.
2. **Self-Awareness**. Know precisely what and how learning is taking place.
3. **Choice**. Choose learning resources whenever possible.
4. **Exploration**. Freedom to sample learning across subjects and disciplines.
5. **Achievement**. Invest more time for higher level of achievements (if desired).
6. **Maturity**. Willing to accept responsibility for learning.

According to a Pew Research survey, seventy-two percent of American adult workers say 'a lot' of responsibility is on individuals to make sure that they have the right skills and education. So, the questions are: What age or stage should a learner take responsibility? How does a learner bear the responsibility?

Always been a proponent of learner centric applications. In the design of the Skills-Based Approach smartphone app, the layout, functionality, and aesthetics are geared for the students. The app puts students in control of their skill sets and lets them manage their tasks, objectives, platforms, and credentials (referenced in stages). With learning labels, a primary objective is to always have students reading and interpreting the labels and then letting them choose what to do whenever possible. Let them navigate through a series of labels based on performance. And finally, with Skills Culture, keeping students aware of best practices in applying skills in their experiences.

Again, I understand the role of education institutions in guiding their students through their learning programs. The learning labels system includes a significant administrative interface for teachers, professors, and institutions to build their learning plans. Once in place, the system gets students in K-16 and workers aware of what and how they are learning, gives them choice when possible, and incorporates personalized learning.

One Uniform Expression of Learning Expectations (v 2.0)

Regarding the adoption of technologies, education and higher education is highly fragmented. Learning labels relate to three specific technologies: learning management systems (LMS), platforms of education publishers, and credentialing systems. It is also worth understanding what and how standards are being adopted. Teachers and professors are inundated with new technologies and applications. What are their decision points in adopting them? Many of these technologies are expanding their commitment levels, from projects to curriculums to grades – this will have future impact.

Learning labels are meant to work with LMSs, not compete with them. Currently, labels work ideally with Google Classroom – a single click button for an assignment. Similar integration with the other LMSs is possible.

How do we track the learning across systems? How do we manage learning across education stages? An advantage of the learning labels technology is tracking learning regardless of the systems, stages, or standards.

Each of the major education publishers (Wiley, Cengage, McGraw, Pearson, and Houghton) is creating their own systems to manage the education resources for their education and higher education markets. (Not surprised by McGraw and Cengage consolidating, combine their resources and systems. They are going after a K-16 market.) An interesting dynamic is how much teachers and professors get locked into a curriculum provided by these publishers.

How do teachers or professors compare curriculums or specific resources offered by different publishers? In either situation, learning labels is an ideal platform to make a basis of comparison decisions and track the learning across publishers.

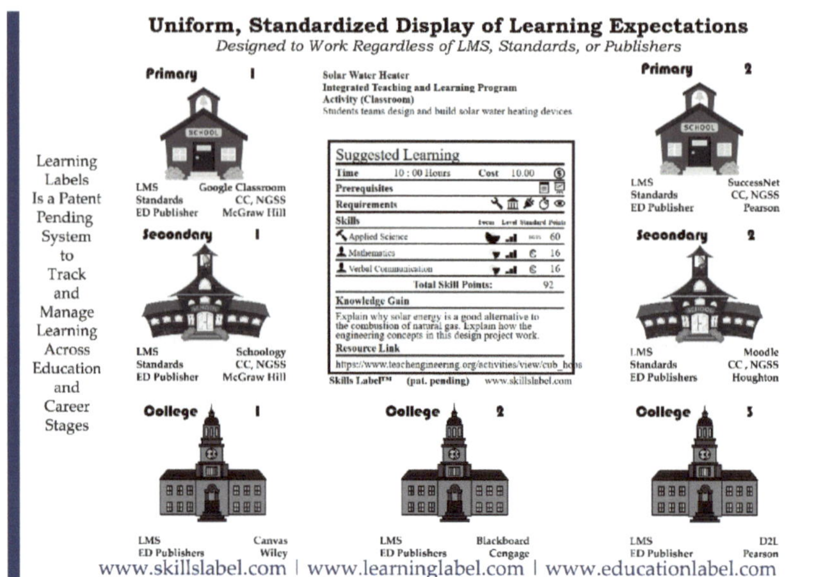

Measuring Learning on a Micro Level (v 2.0)

In science, we miniaturize to get a better understanding of how stuff works. Each time we get smaller, there are new possibilities on understanding how systems works. The same can be said in how we think about learning development and more specifically skills development. This is happening in two ways: understanding the methods and applications behind skills; and breaking down learning into granular tasks. Let's explore the latter.

Traditional education and career planning approaches look two to five years in the future. This type of planning is still worthwhile. For many professions it takes years to materialize and thinking in skills allows for a person to pivot at any time. But to narrow the focus, let's simply start with a task and a desired skill level then move through a series of tasks based on performance and choice. This personalizes the experience, introduces some spontaneity, and makes the learning process adaptive – all on a granular level. This is supported by the learning labels technology.

Learning involves setting goals, creating an environment, taking next steps, and tracking learning. It is possible to get on a task level. Instead of relying on the student or learner, much of next actions can be built into a system. A practitioner maps 'next steps' based on learners' performance.

Let's represent 'real-time' skill competencies. In every experience, learners are applying skills – constantly adding breadth and depth to their skill set. It is possible to track thinking, soft, and multi-disciplinary skills – particularly when they are not the focal point. One feature of the learning labels technology is a Skills Emblem – a dynamic learning badge, where 'real time' learning gains are represented.

Some of the reasons to consider micro-learning:

- Skills are expiring faster, so constant re skilling and upskills is a requirement.

- New faster, efficient ways to get skills.
- Movement towards project-based work defined in skills (not degrees).

Search to Find, Compare, and Consume Education Resources (v2.1)

As a standard representation of expectations for a single unit of learning, a learning label is an ideal node for a search engine. The results of this search, a collection of learning labels, is the best way to makes basis of comparison decisions between labels, evaluate the return on investment of resources, and understand the learning expectations (with or without standards). There is significant perceived value in a search engine with enough learning labels in the system. There are a few ways content gets into the learning labels system:

Content providers index their resources with learning labels. The content might include books (print, online, or interactive), games (online, console, or gamification), activities (online, classroom, or other), projects (series of tasks), virtual reality, etc.

Teacher and professors create labels for assignments, tasks, and projects in their courses. Through this grassroots process, labels get shared among a community of educators and trainers.

Providers of education, higher education, and training standards (and content providers) create labels for resources which properly represent their standards. A search is an effective way to find their standards. Learning labels are ideal for assigning and showing any set of standards.

A basic search is built and online. The current algorithm returns a SERP based on information collected in a learning label: fields / subjects, skills, standards, audience, etc. With more content, sophisticated functionality gets added to the search algorithm, like ranking, suggestive AI, and personalization.

A smart, intuitive interface to contain the results of a search is fully implemented. A collection of labels gets returned in a smart, futuristic dashboard with drag and drop functionality and an easy way to toggle between tiles (ROI), labels (expectations), and credentials.

Whether for an online community of teachers to share learning resources, a platform for education publishers to market their products, or framework for standard providers to circulate their standards, an effective search with the learning label system is a worthwhile feature.

Subject and Skills Searches (v 2.2)

Typically, you search on a subject or field of interest to find learning resources. There is a full context-based search with the learning labels application and further planned functionality. But what if instead, you search on desired skill sets?

There is now another, separate search targeting this functionality. This search function is more relevant for certain types of resources, like online and console games, interactive books, VR experiences, and all kinds of activities or projects – where there is an emphasis on applied learning.

The current learning labels system is well suited to manage the two components of knowledge: facts and information (perspective); and skills. The first, subject matter, gets covered in different fields: like a knowledge gain, standards, and a skills context field. And there is a rich, deep integration in defining skills and their methods and standards.

There is a progression in learning subjects (which might be the biggest concern from learning practitioners); for example, first you take Micro-Economics, then Macro-Economics, and finally an Economics Strategy course. For these courses, there is an umbrella 'economic analysis' skill. Though each includes their own unique skills: Micro-Economics (Problem Solving), Macro-Economics (Policy and Analytical Thinking) and Economic Strategy (Critical

Thinking and Business Strategy). Beyond supporting referencing slightly different skill sets, learning labels also support progression in two ways: create series of labels and reference all prerequisites on a label.

I do not have the research to back precisely the effects of searches on skills versus subject matter (yet). My take is to continue the process of defining learning the same way, include all components of knowledge with a learning label. Also, continue evolving both search functions already established on the website. Once there is enough content in the database (learning labels), use both searches, see the differences in the search results. This could answer many questions related to skills:

Are skills truly transferrable? What are some of the most transferrable skills?

Can skills be learned in different ways? Can users find learning resources based on personal needs or preferences?

Are there more effective learning paths to acquire skills? Can users pivot from one field of study to another? How to pivot into another education or career track based on your skills?

Is it possible to just learn skills, and get domain knowledge later? Will the use of intelligent systems and vast amounts of online information elevate the need for skills (and less the need to remember facts and information)?

As said earlier, I am not sure of the answers to these questions yet. I suggest populating the database by defining the learning in skills (using learning labels), then see the skills correlations and the effect of the searches.

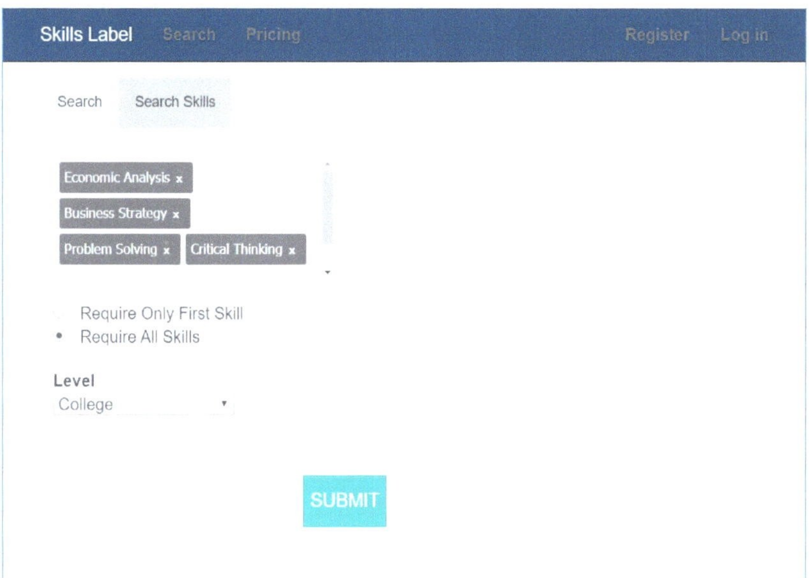

Time to Align Learning Systems to Skills (v 3.1)

The current COVID crisis is a big wrecking ball on our learning institutions, closing schools, colleges, and universities across the country and creating immediate needs: get students learning online (internet access); keep learners engaged; and deal with the effects of social isolation.

The rigidness of our current education and higher education systems is evident by the crisis. (I think) there is too much dependency on a semester (four months) and the credit hour system (time in and out of a classroom). This is the time to explore competency-based learning ("CBL") programs – a movement gaining momentum since around 2014 and more specifically, define learning on a task level, design better pathways, and build 'learner centric' platforms.

Due to the pandemic, some colleges cancelled their Spring semester and others are stressing 'more lenient' grading for online courses (USA Today). The full effect on traditional college programs is uncertain as social gathering could be limited well into the summer. Some questions:

What students get credit for their spring semester? What is the result of students who cannot get the online experience? Is 'lenient' grading fair for preceding students? What is the main goal of education – a degree or job skills? Does the goal change in times of a crisis?

The obvious value in a CBL program is to keep moving students forward once the learning objectives are met; there is no direct linkage to a semester or time.

Define learning on a granular level. Rather than thinking in subjects and semesters, let's define learning in skills, methods and applications, and levels of achievements on a task level – using the exact same education standards already in place. Take a scientific approach: map skills to learning like we map atoms to substances. *Simply aggregate the results to get to a course or project level (where more meaningful learning takes place).*

Create more effective pathways. Of course, one of the big goals in higher education is job preparedness. If we map skills to learning (the first point) and map skills to jobs, then combine the two to create better pathways. (Particularly in this type of crisis, I think the primary goal for professors must be to prepare seniors with jobs skills for a first job.)

Provide more 'learner centric' platforms. Remove the huge dependency students have on teachers and professors for their learning experiences. Put students in the 'driver seat' and let professors take 'co-pilot'.

With these suggestions in place, the higher education system is nimbler. (Worth noting, higher education institutions remain the primary providers, regardless of the system in place.) Learners get more choices with their learning experience as there are more alternatives to get the same set of skills (a benefit of CBL programs and defining tasks in a uniform way). Furthermore, they will be agile, able to pivot into different pathways (tracks) as needed – not encumbered by four-month commitments. Learning labels is an effective system to address each of these suggestions.

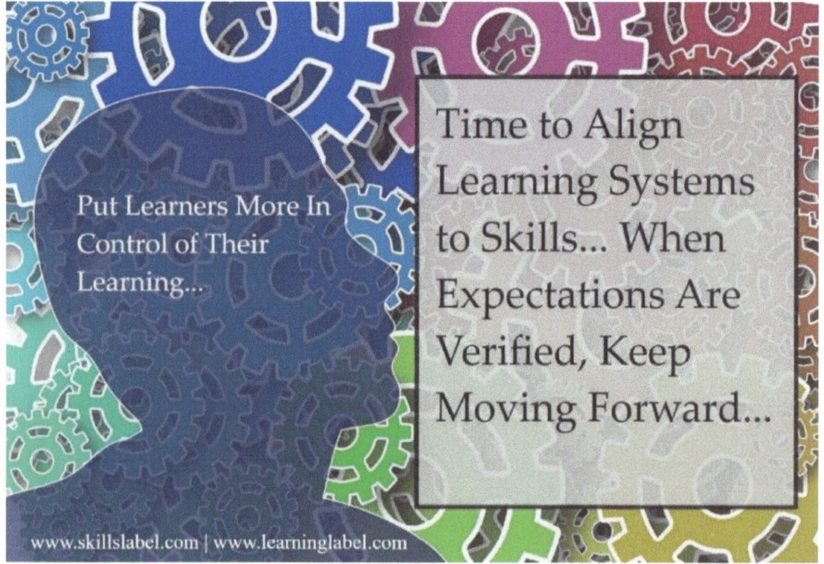

Learning Labels as a Light Learning Management System (LMS) (v 3.1)

As teachers and professors scramble to setup online classrooms due to the COVID crisis, they might feel rushed or forced to adopt a learning management system (LMS). In many cases, the decision is influenced by what their school, college, or university mandates; the LMS might be: Google Classroom, Canvas, Moodle, Blackboard, or a myriad of other ones. I wanted to introduce the learning labels systems as a 'light weight' LMS solution.

The learning labels system includes much of the basic functionality of a LMS. A teacher / professor creates an account in a minute (not requiring institutional support). This is some of the basic functionality (mentioned in previous sections):

- **Create labels.** Defines learning expectations, ROI, and environment for an assignment or task.
- **Create quizzes.** Quick assessments, which are placed before, during, and/or after a task. The system auto grades the submissions.
- **Create badges.** Graphics (PNGs), which get retrieved as expectations are verified.
- **Create lesson plans.** Connect a series of labels together based on performance.
- **Grading.** For tasks which include other assessments (beyond quizzes), there is functionality to grade each learner.

- **Personalized learning.** System supports personalized learning in three ways:
    - Students navigate through a series based on their own performance.
    - Assign tasks directly to students.
    - Assign tasks to a syllabus (course or project). Let students choose (3 of 10, for example).
- **Standards.** Incorporate education, higher education, and training standards into expectations.
- **Dashboard.** Advanced, responsive interface to manage a collection of labels.
- **User Interface.** Similar, simple dashboard for learners to manage their assigned tasks.

But the huge value proposition for learning labels is to *standardize defining and representing learning expectations on a task level* (not necessarily to manage a classroom); in fact, the idea is to get learning labels to work with all LMSs. Currently, there is a single click integration with Google Classroom as an assignment. (The pandemic has provided Google Classroom with a massive boost of more than 50 million downloads recently.)

Furthermore, learning labels are meant to extend beyond teachers and professors creating them for assignments. They define learning for any experience. So, online and print book publishers, VR and game creators, and activity planners build labels for their resources.

The application is designed to have a single learning label for each resource. As professors and teachers find a label that they want to include in a lesson plan, they simply 'clone' the label. This gives them all the above functionality, but they cannot change the underlying learning expectations. Skill Points ®and all the factors supporting the algorithm remain constant.

So, there could be significant upside if the producers of education resources connect with teachers and professors using a common, uniform format – learning labels. In addition, learning labels are readable to all parties – particularly the learners.

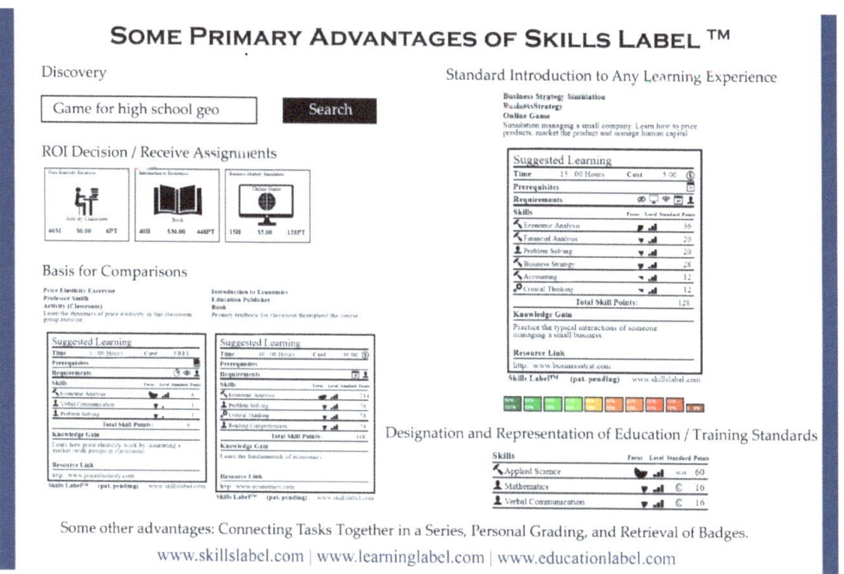

Job Board for Short Term Work (v3.1)

Prior to our current COVID crisis, the economy was moving to shorter term work arrangements. Circa 2009 the term 'Gig Economy' was used to define this type of work. For decades, we see companies moving to 'contract' work; we hear complaints of a prior generation: 'traditional jobs are being outsourced for the bottom line of large companies'. According to a recent 2018 NPR article: "1 in 5 of workers are contract workers"; and labor economists predict "within a decade, freelancers will outnumber full timers".

Freelancing is another term for this short term, project-based work. One 2017 survey from Up Work suggested "36% of Americans are freelancing". BLS survey found: "10% of the American workforce relied on 'alternative employment arrangements'".

There are a number of reasons for the rise of the 'Project Economy'. For workers, project work provides: a second source of income, more job security, a separate career (interests), entrepreneurship, remote capabilities, or a flexible lifestyle. For companies, project work provides: cheaper compensation (because it does not require paying benefits), shorter contractual agreements, and/or appearance on financial documents.

Project based work is often done remotely. This is a statistic of the stark disproportion of access to the 'project economy': "Among workers ages 25 and older, 47% of workers with a bachelor's degree or higher worked from home sometimes, according to BLS data, compared to just 3% of workers with only a high school diploma." (Something worth considering as we struggle through the current crisis.)

As we rebound, I think we are only going to see more of an emphasis on project based and/or contractual work. Moreover, the jobs at larger companies will be one to two-year trials (new hires) or being put on the specific projects of the company (seasoned professionals).

My team is working on an innovative framework for jobs with shorter term commitments. The concept is to populate a number of these jobs in a job board, so workers make easy, line by line, skill by skill comparisons. The 'job label' breaks the job requirements into prior experience and one year 'on the job' application. Also, includes compensation, so a complete ROI snapshot. We are looking for companies posting jobs and job boards to populate this database.

Creating a Better 'Learning Pathway' to a Job (v3.2)

One goal of the learning labels system is to create more effective, efficient learning pathways to jobs; this is accomplished by thinking in skills and reaching set competencies, as opposed to a rigid time-based credit hour and semesters framework found in both education and higher education. In addition, companies (job posters) and education and training providers should use the platform to collaborate in establishing necessary requirements.

The learning labels system includes a hierarchical structure of elements: jobs, courses (syllabus), projects and lesson plans, and tasks (learning labels). One function is to assign elements to their parents (upper levels). So, courses get assigned to jobs, projects get assigned to courses, and tasks get assigned to all the other elements depending on what is required. Someone posting a job uses any of the elements to construct the 'learning pathway'.

Each element gets a unique URL and page to represent the learning and requirements. The learning labels appear as a manageable dashboard on project, syllabus, and jobs. When someone clicks on an element, the learning labels assigned to the element appear colored to mark them.

A company (job poster) might create their own pathway to a job by creating tasks, projects, and courses. This signals to job seekers to complete each of the requirements and when they do, they should get hired for the job. Or, this might be part of an onboarding process: make new hires go through each of the tasks and make a longer-term commitment when they do.

Ideally, a company collaborates with an education or training organization. The company creates a job description (with a job label, showing skills requirements). Then a learning practitioner constructs a 'learning pathway' to address each of the requirements on a job label (or a few of them), might work in conjunction with the company. A few examples:

- A team of professors or learning practitioners at a company create a series of MOOCs with a certificate specifically for a job area, using a collection of job labels.
- A school at a university / college creates a program for a job area.
- A vocational / training institution maps their learning to competency-based learning.
- A learning institution providing a bootcamp, new-age apprenticeship, or micro-credential constructs pathways for their accelerated programs.

And with a healthy number of learning labels, courses, projects, and jobs in the system, learning pathways get constructed as shared resources among a community. An online search within the learning labels system includes a search engine result page ("SERP) with each of the elements. Any party finds the elements and puts them together to construct a learning pathway. Finally, with enough learning pathways, students prepare themselves.

The value in creating 'learning pathways' within the learning labels system is there is complete transparency on a granular level. Essentially, a pathway is built on a 'task' level where all the expectations are clearly represented along with education and training standards to anchor them. Competencies are established by calibrating Skill Points® on an aggregate level. The Skill Points® on a 'job label' should match the sum of Skill Points® in the learning labels for a pathway.

Reputable Companies Are Adopting a Similar Apparatus to Skill Points ® (v3.4)

When you find large reputable companies doing similar work as yours, you know you are doing something right. Recently, I found one such company (the third company so far) creating a remarkably similar apparatus as Skill Points ®; there are the following similarities:

- Name of their product 'Mastery Points', connotes applying and mastering skills.

- Measurements of learning (on a granular level and representing skills).
- Achievement levels and allotments in a numerical form. Similar bars.
- Summing points after completing the work to determine mastery.

This unequivocally proves the relevancy and value of this feature within the learning labels system, which is currently under review at the USPTO. The fact this company already fully integrated this feature into their large content distribution service is significant. They are one of the top providers of free online education and training software in the world.

(I am leaving the names of the companies anonymous and not providing the specifics of their products. I am still in a discovery process. The latest company provides a great product / service with an amazing purpose, a best-case scenario is a collaboration or sharing of resources. Though, Skill Points ® is clearly defined and referenced in 2016 and 2017 patent applications and is an integral feature of the learning label system.)

Of course, there remains some key differentiation features with Skill Points ®, some of them include:

- 1 to 1,000,000 scale for all skills. There are five separate levels within this range.
- Different growth rates for each skill. Calculate skill points on a skill by skill basis. Future research on understanding how skills are learned in education, higher education, and professional development.
- Methodical (scientific) approach in using skill points to define learning and job responsibilities (like coefficients and atoms define substances).
- Direct connection of learning expectations with job requirements. Same Skill Points are used with learning and job labels. Create learning pathways to reached desired aggregates for jobs.

All companies are constantly thinking of new ideas to cultivate their products. It is difficult to identify who and when an organization copies, pirates, or simply comes up with a similar idea. Personally, I think the best approach to get 'credit for an idea' is to put the idea in the public domain and get copyright privileges (maybe calibrating the release with how you choose to use or apply the idea). This article by Syracuse University illustrates releasing an idea this way: A System and Method for Tracking and Managing Skills: TCLC Helps a Rochester Entrepreneur Protect a Bright Idea

When companies copy or pirate a process or utility, there is more at stake because both entities invested their time and resources in developing and moving forward with ideas. Therefore, there are patents and trade secrets. Again, if you feel a company is copying your process or utility you developed, there is clear value in what you are doing and you should feel some flattery (at least that is what my legal team tells me).

To be clear, with the learning labels, here is the relationship between the idea and the utility:

"bright idea: create a standardized representation for learning (analogous to a label for food or resume for experiences)"... "the utility: create learning labels, define learning in skills, reference standards, measure learning with Skill Points, and deliver to an audience; a system to manage and track skills."

Skills Emblem

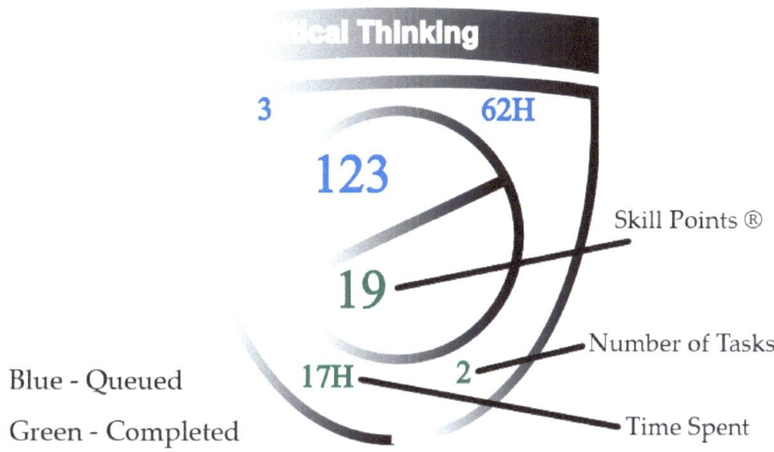

Figure 3 Skills Emblem - Graphic Representation of Skill Points ® for a Single Skill (Critical Thinking). Skill Points ® are summed as tasks are completed. All skills require 1,000,000 points to master and get varying growth rates.

A Pitch in Adopting Skills Applications for Workforce and Skill Initiatives (v3.4)

Before the COVID crisis, there were already a number of proposed workforce and skills initiatives. They were meant to address two much publicized skills gaps: one for the 'new' blue-collar (jobs not requiring a four-year degree); and the one for technical jobs.

Through the crisis, there is increased urgency with these initiatives due to the massive loss of jobs from the crisis. Worth noting the crisis disproportionately hit 'blue collar' jobs, where workers cannot work remotely. Many top technical companies were hiring during the crisis.

There is also some influence from higher education, which was forced to move predominantly online and, at a minimum, commit to a future of blended leaning programs (classroom and online). I argue this is the time to move to programs based on competency-based programs (reach desired skill achievements) as opposed to the traditional time rooted programs (based on six-month semesters and credit hours).

Started to think how I would propose using my platform Skills-Based Approach (the methodology), Skills Culture (the growth mindset), and Skills Label (the system) for one of the initiatives. I would propose the following:

1) Give learners, workers, and practitioners a copy of the book 'A Skills Based Approach to Developing a Career' at cost or free. The book was first published in 2013. I am in the process of editing a newer version of this well-established methodology, which should be ready for this type of release.
2) Promote the adoption of the Skills Culture growth mindset to learning and personal development. The ethos is: "Every Experience is an Opportunity to Apply Skills." Use the

already established online community to share best practices in blogs, articles, and other resources.

3) Get the key learning institutions (high school education, higher education, and training) mapping skills to their programs. The Skills Label system fully supports this process on a task, project, and course level and using any type of education and training standards.
4) Get the key employers 'mapping skills to jobs'. The Skills Label system allows for assigning skills to jobs descriptions, both in prior experience and first year application. Provides a job board of job labels.
5) Create more effective pathways. The Skills Label system allows for matching learning expectations (learning labels) with job descriptions (job labels) to establish pathways. Skill Points ® is a next generation learning measurement that is used on both labels.

Altogether, the platform combines theory with practice and application. There would be some time, cost, and research to prepare the platform for an initiative. Might take a semester for learning institutions to create labels for the tasks and projects in their courses. Employers need to get acclimated to taking an almost scientific approach to defining skills to jobs. There is a lot of research suggested in improving the Skills Points ® 2.0 algorithm; the goal is to sum the points on learning labels to match prior experience or project readiness for first year application on a job label.

But, in ten years, my team created three established resources: a book, patent, and community. All of them are fully supported with an online presence – a website, social media, and search recognition. The Skills Label system is built, went through two formal UI tests during spring semesters and years of refinement.

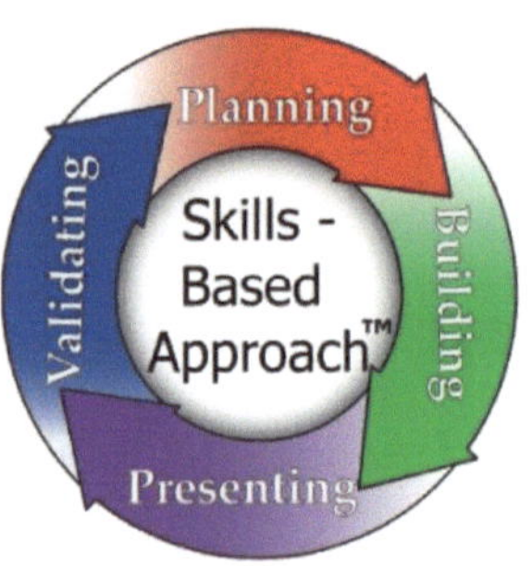

System Pervasive Across Platforms and Devices (v 4.0)

A common theme of this book is learning and job labels set a standard of learning expectations and job requirements, respectively. Another one is learning pathways and dashboards connect them together. To accomplish these two themes, beyond being centered on skills, a system should work across platforms and devices. There are advantages in creating native first applications beyond a substantial web presence and not choosing one platform from another (Android versus Windows 10 versus IOS); all should work together. There are a few good reasons why.

One suggested use of learning labels is tasking, a way to manage tasks, projects and lesson plans, both from the perspective of a practitioner and a learner. With a learner, much of the tasking is accomplished on a mobile device (or smartphone). Like managing email or messaging, the interaction might be as often as five or ten minutes during a learning experience. A learner might be sitting at a tablet, desktop or laptop doing the same (tasking) and/or setting up the tasking (to access on a mobile later).

Another use for a learner is doing immersive learning from a myriad of devices, which requires navigating between the learning definition (labels) and the actual platform providing the content (online course, game, books, etc.). It is more efficient to stay on the same device and platform through this interaction. For example, navigating from a learning label defining expectations in an Xbox game.

Finally, the only option to reach a learner is to create an application for the device. This is not in place at this stage (though designed), but an example would be an app for a smartwatch. A learner moves through a series of learning labels represented as tiles on a smartwatch to either prep or consider purchasing a learning resource.

With a practitioner, there is perceived value in constructing a lesson plan or project as the inspiration hits. For example, a teacher or professor might think of a task for a student or group of students before, during, or after a class. Simply access the application from a mobile device and make the assignment. Similarly, practitioners craft pathways (larger learning objectives – like a course or job) by adding and removing tasks piecemeal.

This could get to a discrete level, what some learning designers call micro- learning or credentialing – an interval of five minutes or less. A label is designed to represent any single unit of learning. Give access to these learning definitions anytime, with whatever device they are using.

On the other spectrum, practitioners are going to setup their learning dashboards and pathways from a large screen. Make full usage of a larger screen display at home or in their office. One reason for the development of the Windows 10 apps for learners and practitioners is to reach them while on a larger screen with a quick, intuitive dashboard.

A good web application accomplishes many of these objectives. Optimize the application for large screens (expand to the full height and width of the screen) and tablets and smartphones (touch enabled). And all of this achieved with the current learning labels web application.

But there are clear advantages in building applications native to the device, such as: saving interactions and settings, sharing resources, building quicker and smarter interfaces, designing better styling and functionality, and using more direct navigation. Many of these advantages overlap across devices and their native platforms. For example, Android and IOS are used on smartphones, tablets, and smartwatches. Windows 10 is mainly used on tablets, desktop and laptops, and Xbox devices. There are currently five Google Android Apps and two Microsoft Windows 10 Apps; there is future planned development for IOS apps too (in a similar structure as the Android Apps). Later versions of the learning labels apps will get deeper by interfacing with the stalwart apps on the system, like Google Classroom and Schoolwork.

One proposed attribute of the learning labels system is a central ledger to keep track of skills outside the confines of the resource itself. Someone playing a game, particularly one where learning takes place, could *get credit* and *store a reference* or link to a completed task. Much of this can be accomplished using a web and API interface, though a smoother interface where resources are shared is possible using the same platform.

A feature in two of the current apps is to conduct a peer review of a resource (represented as a learning label). Ideally, this occurs while a practitioner is using the resource, and this is built into the design of the app. A practitioner might be on a tablet or computer (conduct the review on the same device) or multitasking with two devices to conduct the review.

In the learner apps, there are Skill Emblems – a graphic (PNG) summarizing in queue and completed learning on a skill-by-skill basis (as shown in graphic). A future use of these images (calculated real-time) is to signal skill achievements by sharing them in social media profiles.

More specifically, here are some benefits in working on some of these platforms:

Google – given the dominant position of Android apps, Google Classroom, YouTube (content delivery), and its Search Engine. Earlier the argument is made why learning labels should be accessible on all mobile devices (see graphic for example of current screenshot from Learning Labels Collection and Learning Labels Dashboard – already in the Google Play store).

Microsoft – given the dominant position of Windows 10 on desktops, Xbox, and access to education. The two current applications are directed at practitioners and learners, separately. There is significant functionality in the two apps. They are optimized for larger screens and processing and workable on smaller Surface tablets.

Apple - given the dominant position of IOS apps, iPhone and iPad, a Schoolwork app, and content delivery. Many schools are adopting Apple hardware exclusively for their classrooms. Many of the same arguments for developing Google applications are the same for Apple applications; in fact, many of the basic designs / layouts are the same.

Amazon – given their dominance in the commercialization of learning resources and Android Apps. Learning labels provide a complete ROI to consume a resource. The return is Skill Points. The investment is in time and cost. The dashboard is an ideal platform to make basis of comparison decisions. Both arguments are well established in the patent applications.

At the time in writing this book, there are no current or planned partnerships with any of these companies. All these companies are good targets because they have cloud services, platform for apps and games, invest in machine learning and AI, and provide services to education, higher education, and training institutions.

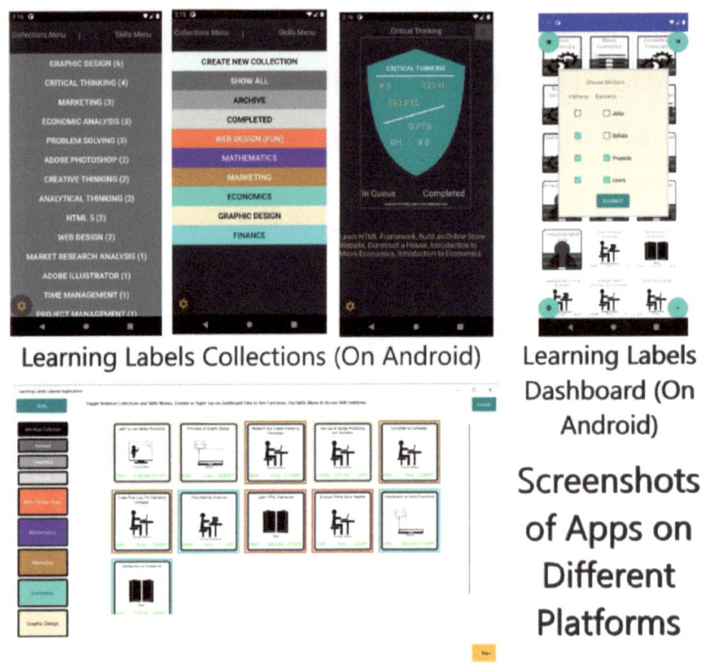

Learning Labels Collections (On Android)

Learning Labels Dashboard (On Android)

Screenshots of Apps on Different Platforms

Learning Labels Learner Application (On Windows 10)

Linking Learning Expectations with Job Requirements (v 4.0)

Skills are ideal for not only defining learning expectations, but also job requirements and both suggest a new paradigm. For learning, the argument is to build a framework around the actionable part of knowledge and a system that changes with the constant churn in learning objectives. For jobs, the argument is practicality – define job preparedness and a way to track lifelong reskilling and upskilling. A job label includes skill definitions for experience (preparedness) and first year application.

The learning label system contains five elements, four of them connect in a hierarchical structure. From top to bottom, they are jobs, courses (syllabus), projects or lesson plans, and tasks or experiences (learning labels). A parent accepts assignments from any of its children. The other element is learners (students or workers). Learners accept direct assignments (personal lesson plans).

The application includes an interface to define each of the elements, which includes features unique to the element. A job and syllabus include composition fields to match industry recognized formats. Once added into the system, each element gets a unique webpage; this establishes full transparency. The landing page also includes unique functionality. For example, a syllabus gets a printable PDF and a learning labels get links to a peer review, flashcards, QR code, etc.

Once an element is defined, it appears in a dashboard and is assignable to a pathway. In the web application, there is a structured and pure dashboard. The latter is simply showing elements freely in the dashboard based on a sort order (not necessarily by the type of element). The dashboard is also in the different apps. To make an assignment, simply drag an element onto the target element.

When an assignment is made, the summary information for target element gets updated (real-time, flickers like a stock price). The four main skill fields are: number of tasks, hours, and skills and total sum of skill points.

A practitioner chooses what sections appear on the dashboard. In a full pathway, one that connects jobs to tasks, there might be many different practitioners working on the elements. Here are some scenarios:

For a university or college, a teacher or professor uses learning labels, project lesson plans, and syllabus to create content for a course(s). A dean, curriculum designer, or career center director uses the syllabus and jobs (maybe projects) to define requirements for specific jobs being targeted by the institution.

For a high school, like above, a teacher uses the labels and projects (maybe syllabus for older students). A principal or superintendent uses the definitions to define requirements for jobs (not requiring a college degree) and degrees.

For an education publisher or game creator, they might only use the learning labels and projects to define learning in their resources. Their learning definitions get incorporated into the projects and lesson plans of teachers and professors.

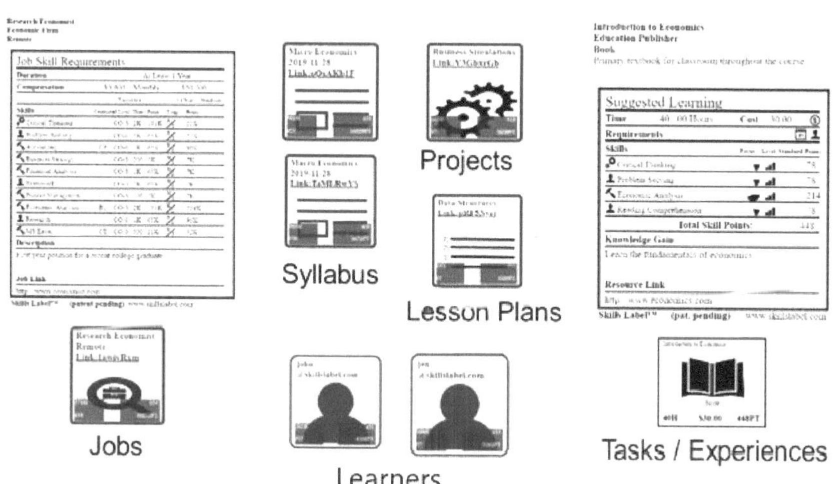

For workforce development, counselors or directors use the syllabi and projects to match the demands of employers in and around the community. To get the definitions, they might partner with the learning institutions in the area they represent. Or there are enough learning labels in the public domain to construct their own higher-level definitions.

Current Functionality

Connecting Learning Labels in a Series

Connect learning labels in a series based on users' performance. A creator of education resources, teacher, or professor chooses the number of outcomes and then assigns labels for each of them. This effectively allows a perpetual series of labels, which can be used for project-based learning, lesson plans, or setting up tasks for a course.

The user (a student or professional) simply clicks on the bar representing their performance and is taken to the next label. Then the next label also has its own set of performance links, effectively connecting the labels together in a series.

This is personal. The scenarios are determined on how the student performs in the learning experience, so next steps are tied to individual performance.

This promotes project-based learning (PBL) and deeper learning. One implementation of PBL is a series of tasks with conditionals, precisely what is accomplished with this functionality.

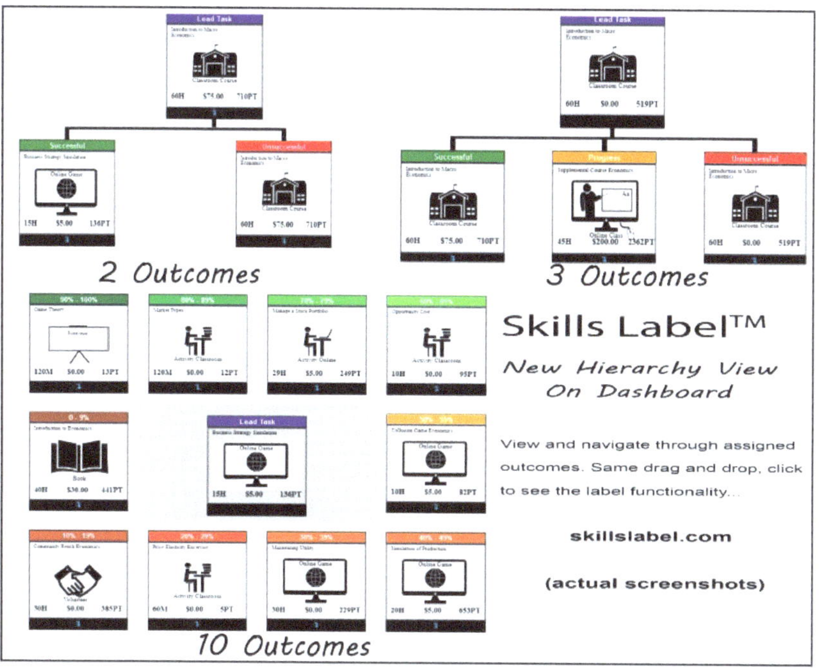

Significant data is collected from a series of labels and could be a source of future iterations and features. But, for now, a human (teacher, professor, etc.) controls what happens with each of the outcomes and creates their own series. This is ideal for a teacher or professor creating and assigning tasks to a course, or a company moving through an onboarding process.

Personalized Grading

Practitioners must be convinced of the need to track learning on a granular level – a task level. To accomplish this, there needs to be a mechanism and navigation to connect learning labels into a series

– so they represent a project, learning plan, or course. This was the biggest influence in adding personalized grading to the application. ***It is possible to create a series of labels, connect them based on performance, and grade each learner. Then, a learner navigates through the series based on their achievements.***

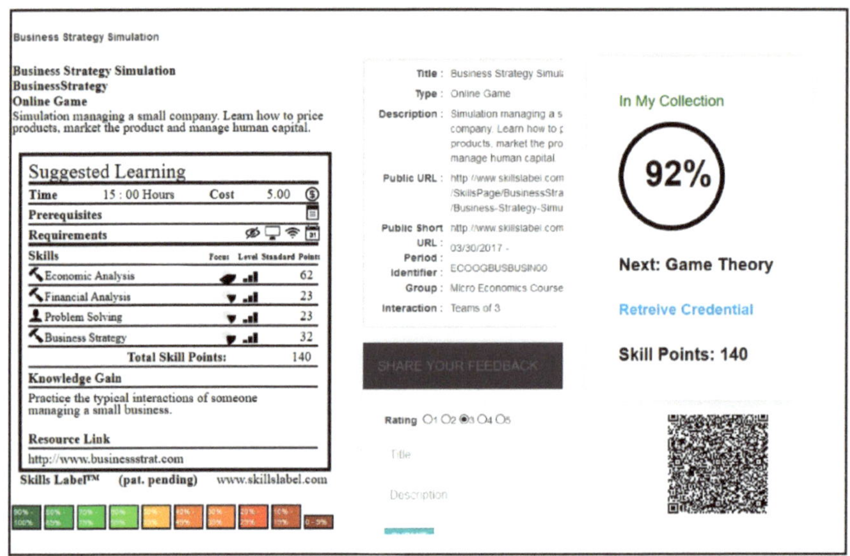

Figure 4 Personalized Grading

Adding grading is useful for other reasons:

- When a learning objective is met, if there is assigned credential, a user gets the credential. After completing a task or series of tasks, a user gets a badge or certification.

- Similarly, a learner earns the allotted Skill Points®. Over time a learner collects Skills Points®. (Future game like mechanics, such as leaderboards, could be added to the system.)

Ways to Distribute Labels (v 2.0)

One goal in making learning labels an effective standard display is to provide many ways to distribute them. Each learning label gets a landing page with its own unique URL. From this page, learning practitioners get learning labels to their audience (learners) in many ways:

1. The label itself is supported in many different file formats (SVG, HMTL, PDF, and PNG). These files can be downloaded and then sent to an audience. There are advantages in using specific file formats.
2. Use an EMBED tag to put a label on a website.
3. Import the label directly into a learning management system ("LMS"). Currently, the application supports a 'one-click' import into Google Classroom. Though, copying the unique URL into the LMS should work with most LMSs.
4. Send the label as an email by clicking on an email.

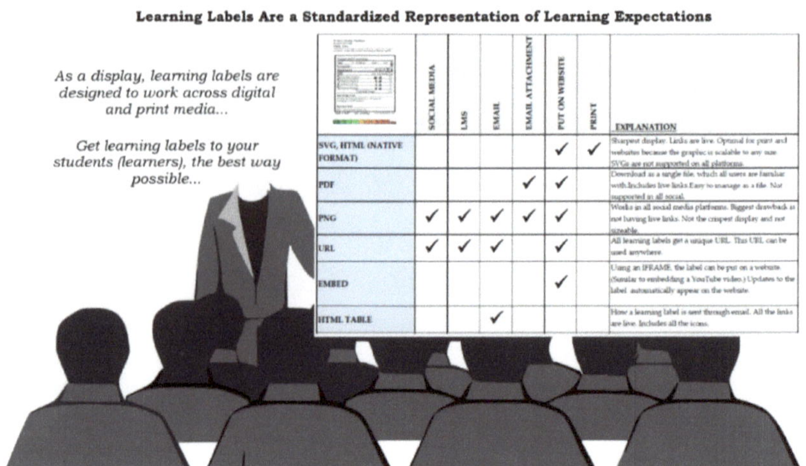

	SOCIAL MEDIA	LMS	EMAIL	EMAIL ATTACHMENT	PUT ON WEBSITE	PRINT	EXPLANATION
SVG, HTML (NATIVE FORMAT)					✓	✓	Sharpest display. Links are live. Optimal for print and websites because the graphic is scalable to any size. SVGs are not supported on all platforms.
PDF				✓	✓		Download as a single file, which all users are familiar with.Includes live links.Easy to manage as a file. Not supported in all social.
PNG	✓	✓	✓	✓	✓		Works in all social media platforms. Biggest drawback is not having live links. Not the crispest display and not sizeable.
URL	✓	✓	✓		✓		All learning labels get a unique URL. This URL can be used anywhere.
EMBED					✓		Using an IFRAME, the label can be put on a website. (Similar to embedding a YouTube video.) Updates to the label automatically appear on the website.
HTML TABLE			✓				How a learning label is sent through email. All the links are live. Includes all the icons.

Learning Label and Standards

No use in having education or training standards without representing them in a clear concise way. A learning label accomplishes this as a uniform display to show learning expectations with standards. The succinctness and readability for all parties (from a child to an adult) differentiates the technology from anything else in the marketplace.

Standards were introduced to learning labels early in the design process. They anchor the learning expectations. Integrating standards is clearly stated on the patent application filed in 2016. The functionality makes learning standards easy to find and assign through the administrative interface and shows them on the labels themselves.

First Common Core standards were introduced to the application. Then dynamic standards, where groups of teachers, professors, or trainers create their own set of standards, were introduced. Then Next Generation Science Standards (NGSS) were added. Importantly, the framework should support most (if not all) relevant learning standards.

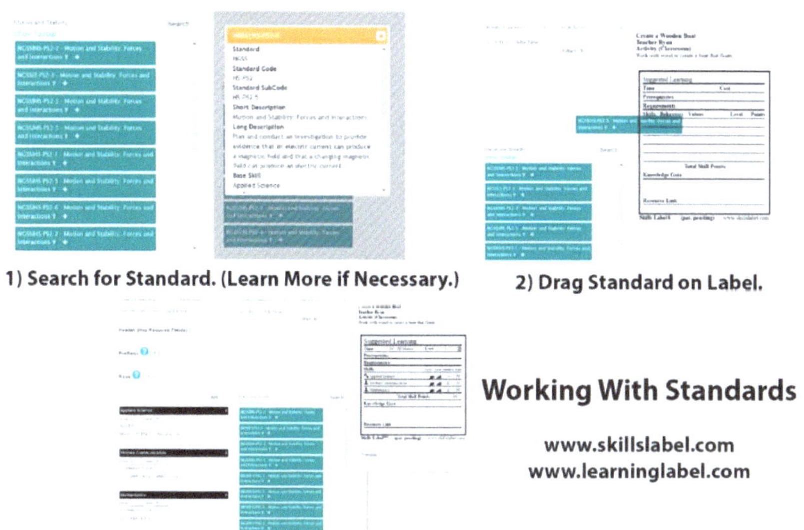

3) See Results. Modify Label to the Activity.

Learning labels are meant to be read and understood by all stakeholders: students, parents, teachers, and practitioners. As said earlier, this is a key differentiator. Competing services listing learning projects, are often page(s) long, difficult to understand, and confusing to make a snap decision to consume the resource. With a learning label, it is possible to understand a learning label in seconds. In the interaction with a label, the participant chooses what to see:

- A young student pays attention to the skills, Skill Points®, how much time it takes, and what they are going to do.
- An older student or parent pays attention to not only what a young student does, but also how much it costs and a generalization of the standards (accomplished by hovering over the standard code on the label).
- A teacher or practitioner pays attention to everything. Perhaps most significantly the standards. (Get a detailed description of the standard by clicking on standard code on the label.)

Assessments (Quizzes) (v 2.0)

There is functionality for taking quizzes within the learning labels framework. This is the basic flow for the learning labels application:

- A learning label is a standard representation of learning expectations.
- An assessment (quiz) verifies what is learned.
- A badge is a graphical credential, which links back to the label.

There is functionality for a learning practitioner to create and give quizzes to their learners at different stages (or segments) in the process. This is probably not much different than Google Forms, or other platforms. The system automatically grades the quizzes and sends the learner to the next task in the series based on their performance. For learners, they access and take the quizzes from the landing page of the learning label.

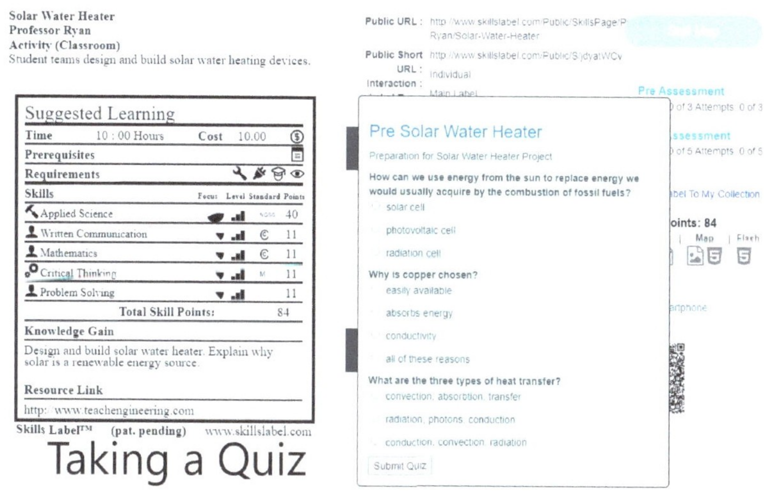

Taking a Quiz

Views (Labels, Maps, and Flashcards) (v 2.0)

In creating a label, there is a significant amount of data collected that can be viewed in different ways – introducing new uses for the technology. An advantage is to use a sophisticated user interface (already built), which includes a smart way to find and assign education, higher education, and training standards to tasks, activities, or experiences and get these views with no duplication of work. There are currently three views: label (default), map, and flashcards.

A learning label remains a standardized representation of learning expectations, useful for learners and learning practitioners in most situations. In no way are these new views meant to take anything from this clear, concise display.

Skill Maps are particularly useful to a practitioner to verify the learning expectations. Simply navigate through each end point, a good framework to verify the learning; this is implemented with the peer review process. Standards provide the basis, so make sure they are accurately represented. A strong attribute of the learning labels is functionality to represent one to many relationships between skills and related standards and methods.

The latest view is Skill Flashcards. The best use for flashcards is to prepare a leaner for an experience. The view has big objects (fonts), colorful (skill types), context and just enough information; the goal is memory cognition, so a learner is guided to apply skills properly in the experience. Might be useful for later reflection. This is different than a task sheet because of the conciseness and more importantly it is not referenced during the experience; let the learner be conscientious and in 'the moment' through the experience.

Each learning label gets a unique landing page with a unique URL. On the landing page, there are links to each of these views (and many other ways to get the views to your audience). In addition, it is possible to toggle between the different views by simply changing the URL. Add the term 'label', 'map', or 'flash' to the end of the URL.

Finally, regardless of the views used, all the functionality of the learning system is useful.

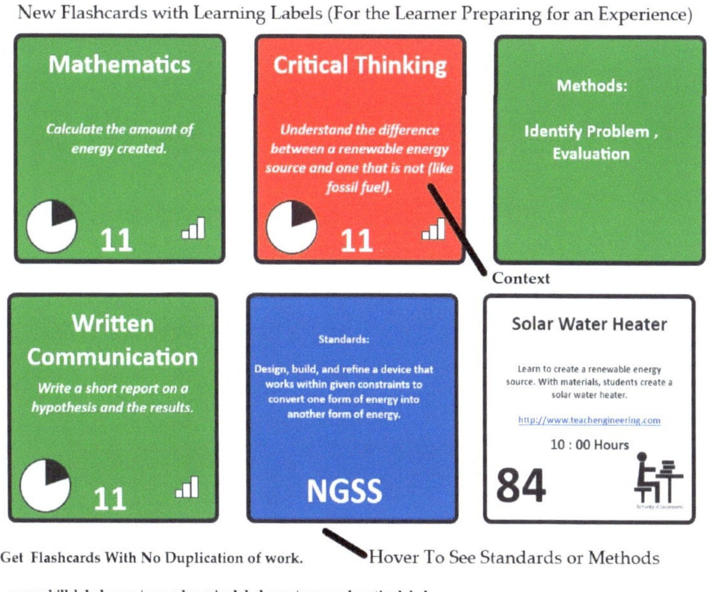

Peer Reviews (v 2.0)

Number one suggestion from practitioners for use and adoption of the learning labels is providing a way to verify the expectations. To them, the process is akin to an accreditation or book review. Many ask the questions: "Who says these learning labels are accurate? How do they conduct a review?".

The learning labels system includes a fully functional process to verify the expectations. Currently, this works as a peer review process, though could be used in other verification processes too. The basic premise is a reviewer checks each end point on a Skill Map (a graphic layout of the traditional label, ideal for these reviews); end points could be a skill, methods, or standards. If they agree with the representation, then check a box and optionally leave a comment.

In addition, a practitioner might use the Skill Map application as they are reviewing the resource and check each time a skill is applied and click and hold to measure the intensity. This can also be accomplished by doing a click and hold for each skill after reviewing the resource (probably more common at first).

The application records all this data and who made the review and their profile information. Later, this can be negotiated for credibility concerns (if necessary). Future iterations might include support for machine learning or AI to aid the reviewer. The process works well for later advancements in this review process.

This line by line check of skill representations makes sense for the following reasons:

First, the verifier might be interested in only the skills in their discipline. For example, a standards provider, might review an experience to ensure it properly applied their standards (and that is all). Might not have the expertise, time, or interest to verify other skills.

Second, verifier goes line by line checking skills as they are applied. Might have the application open as they are reviewing the resource. Might agree to only some of the skills represented on the label.

This framework and thoroughness provide a strong basis to make these learning labels accurate. Skill Points® are a next generation learning measurement. Each variable in the calculation gets verified: level of difficulty (largely based on standards) and focus values (based on the collected frequency and intensity); there are also coefficients based on other factors.

A teacher, professor, or trainer considering using a learning resource (book, game, activity, etc.) views a learning label (represented as a Skill Map), which shows how many practitioners agree to the expectations and the most recent comments (on a skill by skill basis). This is especially useful if standard providers participate in the process too.

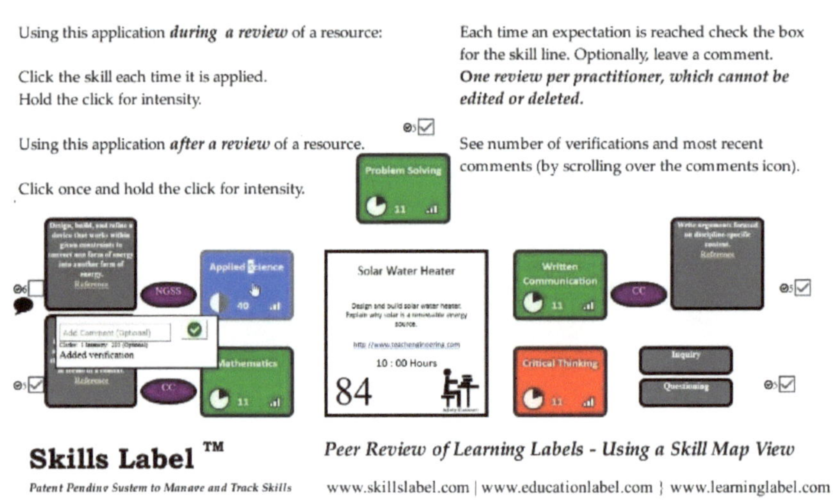

Personalized Learning (v 2.0)

Personalized learning is a popular trend in education, higher education, and professional development. The definition of personalized learning is to craft lesson plans or projects to the learner. A teacher, professor, or mentor assigns tasks based on a learner's abilities and proven skills. The difficulty with personalized learning is it can be a time-consuming process. There are three ways to introduce personal learning with the learning labels technology.

One way is to create a syllabus to represent a course, project, or maybe an onboarding experience (for professionals). This online syllabus (www.skillsyllabi.com) contains all the same fields as a regular syllabus, plus a section to include a collection of learning labels. The idea is to add all relevant tasks where a desired learning achievement is reached and then let learner choose a certain number of them.

One way is to create a personalized learning plan within the dashboard of learning labels application, where tasks are specifically assigned to learners. The intuitive interface makes the process easy to both assign and unassign tasks to individual learners. Once a set of learning labels are in place, takes a matter of seconds to complete a personalized learning plan.

One way is to start learners with a task, then let them navigate through a series of tasks based on their performance – one approach to project based learning. This also introduces adaptive learning (on a task level). There is grading and quizzing functionality to make the navigation process between tasks automatic.

What is valuable about these last two options is that they are ongoing, meaning they can traverse across education and career stages. A teacher, professor, or mentor works with learners if they want to, not bounded by a semester. There are no limits to the how many tasks are in a learning plan or series.

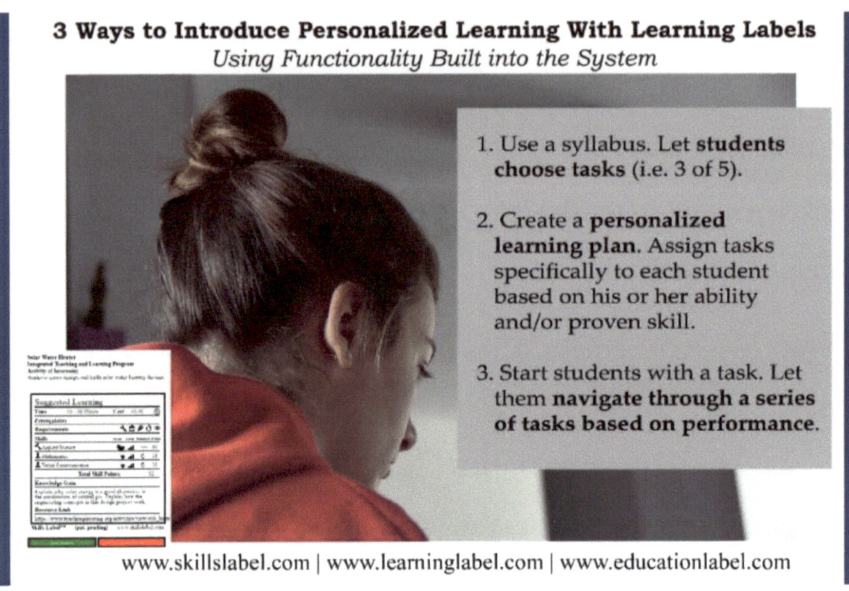

There is a place for collective learning approaches, but also a place for personalized learning approaches. Students and professionals have different interests (passions), values, and skills, so let them explore (choose), stay engaged, and perform – each supported by the learning label technology.

Smart Intuitive Dashboard to Manage a Collection (v2.1)

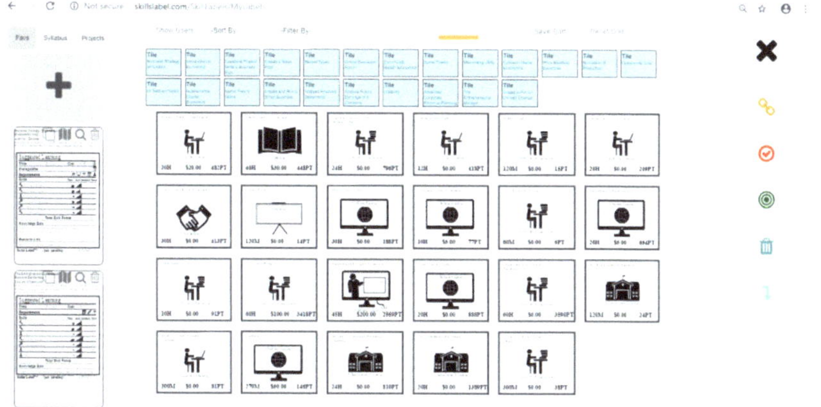

Imagined a smart dashboard to manage learning labels early in the design of the system. First focused on building the standalone learning label, establishing it as the standard representation of a single unit of learning. Then, created an interface to manage a collection of them: a tiled, draggable dashboard. An early version of the dashboard appears as a graphic in the 2016 patent application.

A quote from IBM's CEO saying we are "experiencing the 'net flixifcation' of learning" and the company adopts a "skills culture" motivated me to dramatically improve the learning labels dashboard. It is unclear whether she was referring to Neflix's suggestive AI algorithm or interface for quick decision making of a user. Both are relevant within the context of the learning labels system.

There are three separate versions of the dashboard (each includes functionality targeting the user):

- Teacher (Administrator). Assign tasks to learners, projects, or syllabus. Trigger grading, series, and other functions.
- Learner. Learners manage their workload, current and future tasking.
- Search (SERP). Interface to manage the results of a search.

The idea is to create a single dashboard framework, then modify it to represent the functions of the different versions. Establish a familiarity among all the different users.

The basic dashboard framework includes the following:

1. Toggle between elements. Double-click on tiles (a ROI for a task), labels (expectations and links to resources), and credentials (reward) to see the elements.
2. Draggable elements in the grid. Grid is responsive to changes in size and element representations. Ideal way to see basis of comparison of labels. Create and save sort orders.
3. Draggable elements outside of the grid. Right column includes action icons based on the version. Simply drag an element on an action icon to start the function. Left column

(only on larger screens) includes more sophisticated functions (again, based on the version).

4. Sort menu bar. A set of small tiles represents all the items in the grid. This is useful to establish a sort order for a larger set of labels.
5. Top menu. Includes functions to manage the grid and toggle between the grid and text list layout.
6. Layout of the grid is designed to be fast and efficient. There are no extra functions. For example, there is no standard 'header', 'menu' or 'footer' found on a typical web application.

For the administrative version, there are features in the left and right columns. The left column includes functionality to work with favorites, syllabus, and projects. The right column includes functionality to see a landing page, grade, create a series, and see a hierarchy.

For the search version, there is the same layout. The left column includes functionality for sorting and filtering and a more sophisticated search on skills. The right column includes functionality to see the different views of a label and features for a logged-in user.

Job Descriptions with Skill Points® (v 3.0)

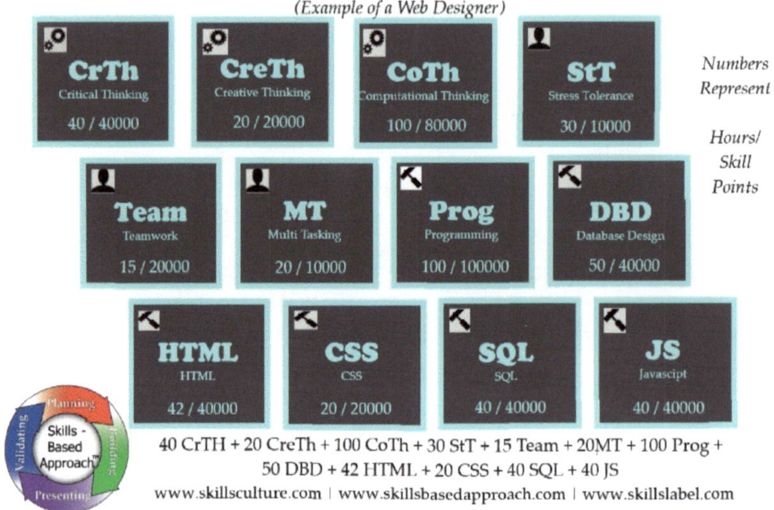

I suggest we use skills to define job requirements and learning expectations like we use atoms to define substances, get deeper by working with standards, methods, and applications (like sub-atomic particles), and calibrate to different levels using a numerical representation (Skill Points ®). Regarding learning, I made this analogy a few times already in this paper; so, in this section, let's see how this works with job requirements.

There is functionality to create a job description within the learning labels system. This is not meant to replace, but rather supplement or augment this well-established format. Many of the standard sections / fields are included, along with a skills section that is designed to get the required information to calculate Skill Points ®. Use the same or a slightly modified algorithm as with the learning labels to calculate Skill Points ®; this works skill by skill, with the same skill growth rates, variables, and coefficients.

The main objective is to connect the learning expressed by the labels with a job description; then, with enough learning labels in place, create learning pathways. This is how the linkage works:

- Quantify required skills for a job, both in experience and first year application, using Skill Points ®.
- Use Skills Label ™ to define learning tasks; quantify learning using Skill Points ®.
- Overlap the job requirements with learning expectations to create effective learning pathways.

The creation of job descriptions is accessible to users with a valid admin account for free. Like with the learning labels, each job description gets a unique landing page and URL. Some other suggested functionality includes:

- Use the same skills interface and features to create learning labels with job descriptions.
- Create learning pathways to get required skills for new hires. Guarantee a job to someone who successfully completes the pathway.

- Create a series of learning labels for the onboarding of a new employee. This is already a suggested feature of this technology.

Finally, I am considering designing a standard display for job descriptions, like a learning label. This would allow for quick basis of comparison decisions on jobs, largely based on experience and first year application of skills. The value proposition is to give early career workers a platform to make quick choices in an increasingly project-based economy. But as said earlier, this type of representation would supplement, deeper job descriptions.

Staff Economist

Economic Firm

Created
2/22/2020 2:09:00 PM
Location
Remote

Sample Job Description For Job After College

A Proprietary Algorithm Calculates Skill Points ®

Skills	Past Experience				First Year			Standards / Methods
	Level	Hours	Credential	Skill Points®	Usage	Hours	Skill Points®	
Critical Thinking	CO-3	1000		2000	Daily	4	2000	
Problem Solving	CO-3	2000		2500	Daily	5	2500	
Economic Analysis	CO-3	1000	Bachelors	2000	Hourly	1	2000	Understand cost of production, supply and demand, and price elasticity
Financial Analysis	CO-3	1000		2000	Daily	2	2000	
Active Listening	CO-0	200		1500	Daily	5	1500	
Teamwork	CO-3	5		1500	Daily	2	1500	Work in teams on a task by task basis
Research	CO-0	2000		2000	Hourly	1	2000	Find, analyze, and synthesize information across many sources
Microsoft Excel	CO-3	200	Microsoft Excel Certification	1000	Hourly	1	1000	Create charts. Aggregate data across sheets. Use pivot tabels
Analytical Thinking	CO-3	100		2000	Hourly	1	2000	

Responsibilities

Conduct Research

One of the Economist's main duties is to research economic issues and trends. Using various methodologies and sources, Economists must be able to obtain recent and relevant data for their employers. The way they go about this will differ depending on the organization they work for and the type of Economist they are. Most Economists utilize the internet to conduct some research, while others seek out peer-reviewed essays and articles. Economists may interview subjects, scan databases or create and administer surveys. The methods abound and most Economists will use a variety of them throughout the course of their career.

Analyze Data

Locating information is just the first half of the Economist's job. Once they find the data they sought, it must still be analyzed or interpreted. Economists spend a great deal of their time making sense of the data they have collected and finding ways to represent their finds. For some this may result in a scientific paper, for others it may take the form of a presentation for management or a forecast report. The job will specify how the Economist is to share the information, but all Economists are tasked with this in some form or another.

Qualifications

- Bachelor's in Business, Economics, or Accounting
- MBA (preferred)
- CPA (optional)

www.skillslabel.com | www.educationlabel.com | www.learninglabel.com

Job Labels (v 3.0)

Introducing new 'job' labels, a standard representation of skills for a job description. Job labels define requirements for prior experience and the first-year application of skills. Like learning labels, jobs labels are an ideal format to make basis of comparison decisions and quickly understand a set to requirements.

Job labels formalize the skills section on the well-established, context driven job description. This is the value in 'job labels' for different worker segments (with enough job labels in the system):

- **Recent college graduate.** Help identify technical skills to work on in the first year. Common skills get matched at the top of the labels. So, for example, a business graduate, who might be interested in sales, economics, or finance jobs, finds precisely what unique skills will be applied in each of them. Use job labels to narrow top choices, then learn more by clicking a link (on the label) to a full job description.
- **Recent high school graduate**. Focus on what skills are applied in the first year in a job. Find jobs where a graduate possesses or can acquire necessary skills. Thinking in skills is advantageous, because they bridge expectations not defined in a degree.

- **Recent certification.** Identify jobs where the certification is relevant. Many 'blue collar' jobs (defined as jobs not requiring a four-year degree) are best defined in skills. (A future goal is to merge the learning and job labels to create better pathways.)
- **Early career professional**. Use job labels to make quick decisions on shorter term commitments. An effective platform for workers to find second or freelance jobs in an increasingly project-based economy.

As a standard representation, job labels are in an ideal format to make line-by-line, skill by skill comparisons. There is established familiarity with learning labels, as the job labels are constructed in a similar format. A collection of job labels, which appears after a search, is shown in a smart, responsive dashboard (like the learning labels). This is an ideal interface to drag the labels into different sort orders and toggle between tiles and jobs.

See a basic example:

1. Go to the website at http://www.skillslabel.com/Search/Search
2. Select 'Job Labels' and search on 'thinking' (a general term across jobs).
3. Double-click on the tile to see the label.
4. Drag the tiles into different sort orders.

The goal is to: map learning to skills; map jobs to skills; and combine to make more effective pathways.

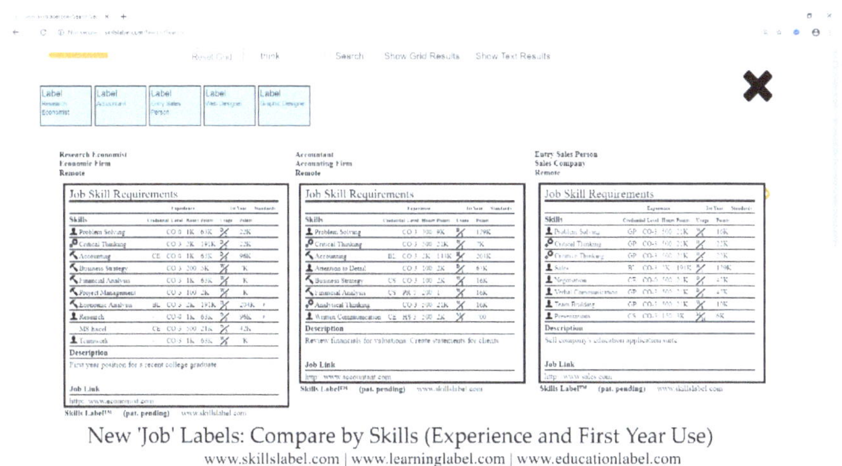

New 'Job' Labels: Compare by Skills (Experience and First Year Use)
www.skillslabel.com | www.learninglabel.com | www.educationlabel.com

Skills Matching Algorithm (v 3.0)

There is a skill matching algorithm for searches returning learning or job labels. On each search, the user chooses skill matching or keeping the default order. With skills matching, the algorithm takes the search result and ranks how the skills appear on each of the labels. The goal is to align the skills for line by line, skill by skill comparisons to aid a reader looking at a collection of labels.

The option for the default order is in place because this order was chosen by the creator of the label. A practitioner prioritizes the importance of skills for the learning expectations or job requirements. For smaller data sets, leaving the default order might be preferable. Also, for users slowing down, taking their time, keeping the prescribed order might also be preferable.

The skills matching algorithm calculates the number of matches skills appear in a collection of labels, the frequency and intensity skills are applied in learning, and sum of skill points in jobs to construct a ranking order. So, the matching is based on a collection of labels, not the actual search term (whether skills or a subject). Currently, there is a separate ranking algorithm for the order learning and job labels appear in the dashboard that is based on the search criteria. There is more planned sophistication for this ranking algorithm (such as personalization), once enough labels are in the database.

This added skill matching functionality is a good example of the effectiveness of the learning and job labels as a dynamic, standard representation. On the client and server side, the labels are readable and updateable. Considering a future feature where there is 'auto skill matching' to the before and after labels when a label is dragged into a new place on the dashboard.

Skill matching makes comparing and interpreting a collection of labels faster and intuitive for a learner or job seeker to make quicker decisions.

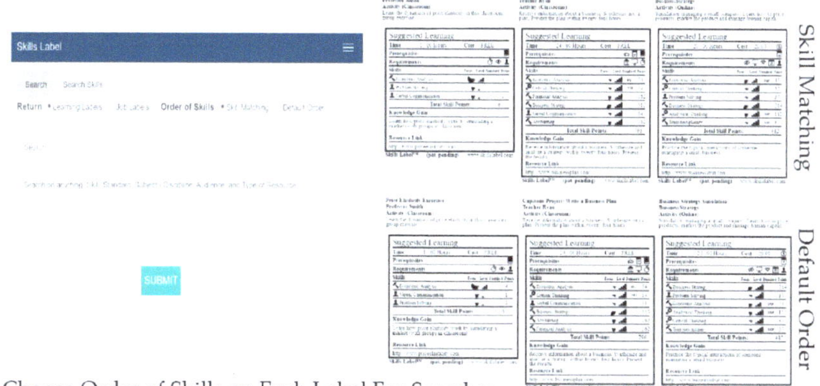

Choose Order of Skills on Each Label For Searches

Colored Dashboard to Manage Four Elements (Jobs, Courses, Projects, and Tasks (v3.3)

To effectively manage the four elements of the learning labels framework, a second dashboard was added to the application. (As referenced in a previous section) the first dashboard is designed to manage a collection of learning labels and all the functions related to learning labels (i.e. grading, series, etc.).

This second dashboard is designed to make assignments for the elements (jobs – job labels, courses – syllabus, projects / lesson plans, and tasks – learning labels); this is accomplished by dragging an element on a parent. Functionality might be added to quickly create new elements, though the general idea is the elements are already created.

On this dashboard, the elements appear in sections stacked on top of each other (a future function is to allow moving the sections into different layouts – i.e. put jobs to the left and syllabus and projects on top). Each of the sections is collapsible – a learning practitioner might not need the jobs section, or a job poster might not need to work with the syllabus section.

All the elements are draggable (except for jobs, which is the top level). An element is dragged on a parent to reference or unreference the element, so: jobs accept syllabus, projects, and tasks; syllabus accept projects and tasks; and projects / lessons plans accept tasks. (To clarify, the difference between a project and lesson plan: a project sets a desired goal where tasks are evolving; and a lesson plan is a list of required tasks.)

Once assignments are made, the user clicks on an element to see all the references with color borders. (As the graphic shows) clicking on a job, related syllabus, projects, and tasks are all highlighted; in the grid of tasks, the colors are propagated by the parent: green represents syllabus, light blue represents projects, and orange represents direct assignment. This makes it easier working with learning labels on an aggregate level.

For transparency, each element in the dashboard includes its unique link (URL) to a landing page. As a user constructs a learning pathway, it is possible to follow the link to see how the element is currently represented online:

- Job page includes a 'job label', which aggregates the experience and first year expectations in a similar format as a learning label. The aggregate should represent what learning is assigned to the job.
- Syllabus page includes all the standard fields of a syllabus, plus added fields referencing skills and a collection of learning labels. A syllabus is viewable as a PDF and learners can choose what tasks to work on.
- Project / lesson plan page includes a definition, standards (if applicable), and a collection of tasks.
- Learning labels page is sophisticated (being the foundation of the system). (See prior section on all the functionality on its landing page.)

The credibility is established on a task level with the learning labels. Each learning label supports designating education and training standards and a complete peer review process. Standards might be referenced on a project. Skill Points® is a next generation learning measurement, which appears on the learning labels. Aggregate ranges might appear on projects, syllabus, and jobs.

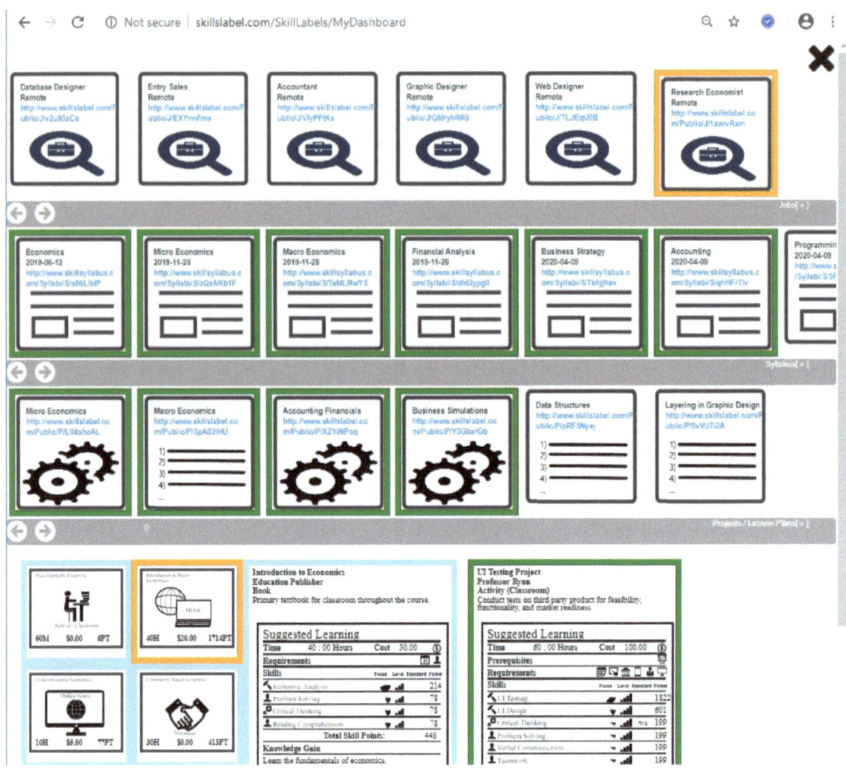

New Parser for Job and Learning Descriptions (Content) Returns Skills (v3.3)

Learning and job labels are not meant to replace the textual, context driven learning and job descriptions. The format of a job description is well established. Instead, I suggest a learner or job seeker narrows down choices by comparing labels, then clicks on a link to view the full description. Regardless, a new parsing feature uses the context in these descriptions to derive skills and related content on the labels.

Some of my general complaints with many of these descriptions: unnecessarily long; lack of quantitative data; and generic. For example, in LinkedIn, a job poster starts the description with already created content. Four value propositions of the labels are:

- Quantifies the expectations and requirements.
- Sets up an interface to make quick comparisons.
- Connects learning expectations with job requirements (pathways).
- Establishes a familiar display (fits on a smartphone screen, no need to scroll up-down or left-right).

Two full spring semesters, I worked with graduate students, professors, and teachers to improve the user interface (through formal testing). The results showed building a label takes around a minute. (My observation watching users in the application) users do not like text entry (particularly with repeat information) and spending time trying to figure out how an interface works.

A new parsing feature speeds up the process and learning curve in using the application. A parser reads a block of content from a URL (website) and/or text copied into a textbox. For a job label, the content is a job description (but could be anything that relates to a job posting). For a learning label, the content could be a review of the learning resource, an online catalogue, or part of a lesson plan.

At this stage, the parser focuses on defining skills from the content fed into the application. The parser looks for direct references to skills and other semantics to suggest matches (such as interests, traits, job attributes, and fields / disciplines). Skills get added to the labels automatically, ranked in an order of match strength.

The next steps are to verify the inclusion of each skill on the label (delete unnecessary options), set the expectations and requirements, add any missing skills, and put them in the sort order to appear on the respective label.

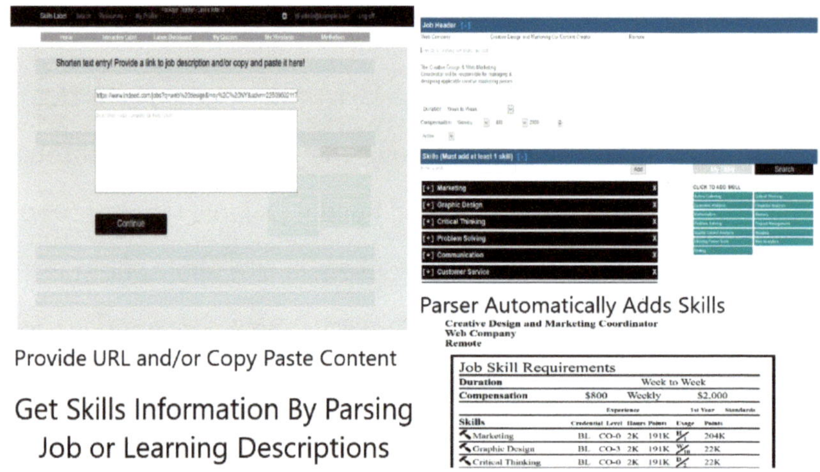

Less Data Entry, Less Time Creating Learning Labels: Context Parser Ranks, Suggests, and Add Skills (v 3.4)

In nine years of application design, I realize users do not like data entry. It is more painful with repeat data. This is not just an obvious blanket observation, but a theme from two formal user interface ("UI") tests with graduate students, professors, and teachers. One of my conclusions from their work is the adoption of my technology depends on how fast users create the results – learning and job labels.

The best way to speed up the process is to limit data entry. In fact, this was one of the key inspirations in creating the learning labels in the first place. I wanted for a single person to create a label, then everyone else gets to use the label in a tasking application. But through the UI testing and watching the creation process, that single person included, does not want to spend much time entering data when he or she can get it from other sources. This was one of the motivations in creating the skills parser (another big motivation is getting better accuracy).

In previous sections, I introduce the parser for job descriptions. There is significant new functionality, such as ranking and parsing a URL. Typically, a learning label should have between four to six skills and no more than ten skills. A job label might include between ten to fifteen skills and no more than twenty skills. The ceiling is set to maintain clarity and precision in representing the skills. So, a parser helps not only in identifying skills but also choosing which ones to add by ranking them.

The parser accepts a URL (website address) and/or a block of content, which gets added by copying and pasting or uploading a file. So, a learning practitioner creating a learning label might use a lesson plan or review, task sheet, or project description. A job poster or recruiter creating a job label might use a job description, job definition (in an employee handbook), or ideal resume. Currently, the parser supports job descriptions as a URL from each of the top job boards.

The parser reads the content/context and returns a ranked list of skills. It accepts two parameters: suggesting or adding the skills automatically; and setting a threshold from low to high. Suggesting is helpful for working through a large set of skills (low threshold) and choosing the most relevant ones. Selecting to add skills automatically works optimally with a medium or high threshold.

Parsing a URL works well with the job boards that provide a single page for the job, like Dice. With Indeed and Monster, finding a page with only a single job is more challenging; therefore, at this stage, copying and pasting from the page gets more accurate results. Though this is an early iteration of the parser; later, the algorithm should get better in accepting URLs.

With suggestions, a section is provided with skills sorted by rank; a user simply clicks on an element to add a skill to the label. When automatically added to the label, the skills appear in a ranked order; a user goes through the list and might delete or add skills and change the order the skills. Either way, a user can scroll over the element and see each of the factors that determine each of the rankings.

This is an early iteration of this feature. My team plans to significantly advance the skills parser with better rankings, more precise results, and add more elements from the parser onto the labels.

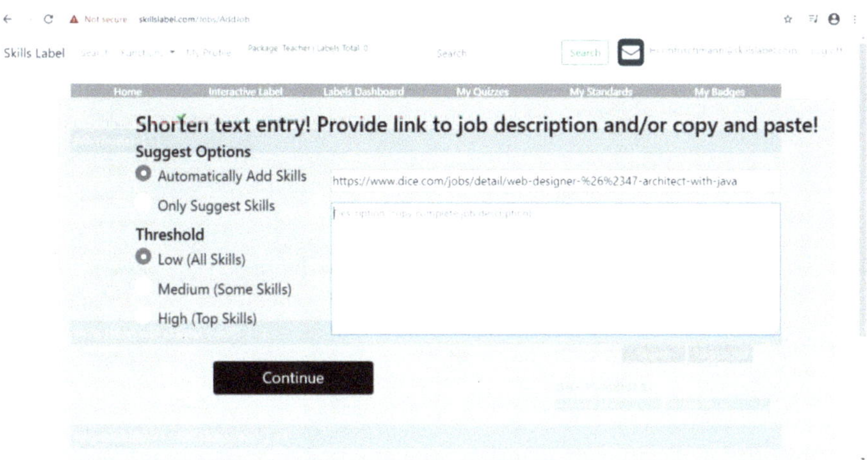

Figure 5 Screen for Parser

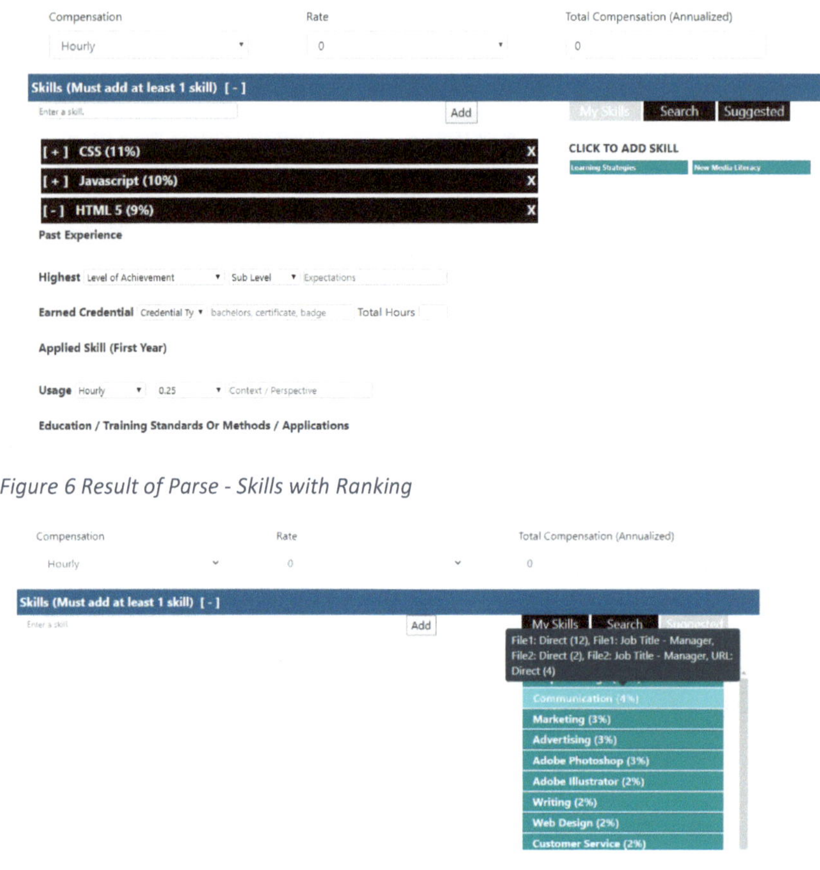

Figure 6 Result of Parse - Skills with Ranking

Figure 7 Scroll over Skill Shows Factors in the Ranking

Building Interoperability with Learning Management, Credentialing, and Publisher Systems (v3.4)

A common theme argued in previous sections is learning labels set a standard for defining learning and therefore should work across various types of learning applications. In most cases, getting applications to work together requires Application Programming Interface (APIs) and/or Learning Tools Interoperability (LTIs).

For some time, there is an interface to create an assignment for Google Classroom within the learning labels system. On the landing page for a label owned by an administrator, there is an icon to create an artifact in this popular learning management system. The process is ideal; the results get better.

A learning label is designed to define learning for a task or project, so fits well within the parameters of an assignment. The current use of the share button works well, though working with the API might allow integration with the learning labels dashboard – an ideal way to make comparisons, which allows learners to make choices. For example, create ten assignments in the learning labels system, import them into Google Classroom, and then let the learners choose three of them using the dashboard.

I am exploring how to use APIs to connect with the popular LMSs like Blackboard, Canvas, Moodle, D2L, etc. The process should be like the one established with this Google Classroom interaction, working with assignments representing tasks or projects.

After reviewing the Blackboard API documentation, the process should be: 1) authenticating a user; 2) retrieving owned courses; 3) creating ‘content’ or ‘group’ assignments for a selected course. Figure this same process should work with other LMSs, simply different authentication procedures.

Here it is also worth mentioning learning labels might work as a standalone ‘light LMS’ (as discussed in another section). There is functionality to put labels in a series, create a syllabus and projects, grading, a dashboard to manage a collection of labels, and support for personalized learning. Some of this functionality is also supported with the API.

The learning labels system is also an ideal why to work with education, higher education, and training standards. Currently, the system works with four sets of national / international standards. I am looking to also establish interoperability with the organization representing the standards. The basic interaction / process would be to find a standard, link them to skills, and post them on a learning label.

Finally, to get other applications to work with the learning labels system, there is currently an API with the following functionality (with a registered administrative account):

- Get all labels for a user.
- Get all the fields for a label.

- Create a label.
- Get all fields for a syllabus.
- Create a syllabus.
- Conduct grading for a task (represented as a label).

I think for an education publisher or game creator, accessing the learning labels API is an ideal way to show and list learning labels representing the artifacts they create within their website and mobile applications.

So, the two goals are to get the learning labels application to work with partner applications and vice versa. For the first goal, looking to get access to third-party platforms to use a collection of learning labels. For the second goal, looking to build awareness and open access to the learning labels system.

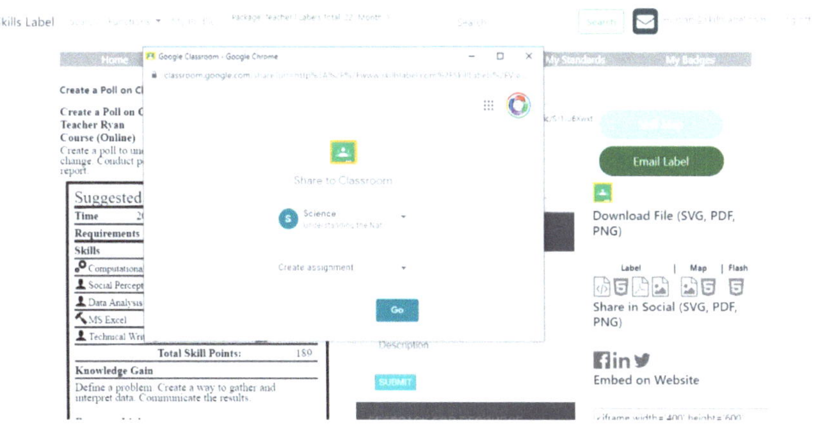

Figure 8 Show Google Classroom to Add Label as an Assignment

Learning Label Pathways and Dashboards (v 4.0)

With the learning labels system, there are learning dashboards and pathways. Dashboards are designed to be a responsive, drag and drop grids with pre-specified elements represented as tiles and put into a sort order. Pathways are direct assignments connecting the elements together; they include recorded tasks and summary of skill data represented by the learning labels.

A dashboard might represent a personal or group lesson plan, a project, class, course, job track, training module, etc. The use case is to setup scenarios where a practitioner responds to the experience. For example, as a worker goes through an onboarding process, a practitioner adds and removes tasks from the dashboard based on his or her performance. Or a teacher might setup a dashboard with students and tasks for a future class.

A learning pathway is threaded across platforms and possibly practitioners to achieve a goal. This might be getting a job, exploring career paths, personal growth, a degree or education, and reskilling and upskilling workers. A practitioner sets up elements as a dashboard, then reference the dashboard in constructing the pathway.

A pathway in the context of the learning labels system is less static than a degree. This is clear by the ease in adding and removing the elements from the dashboard.

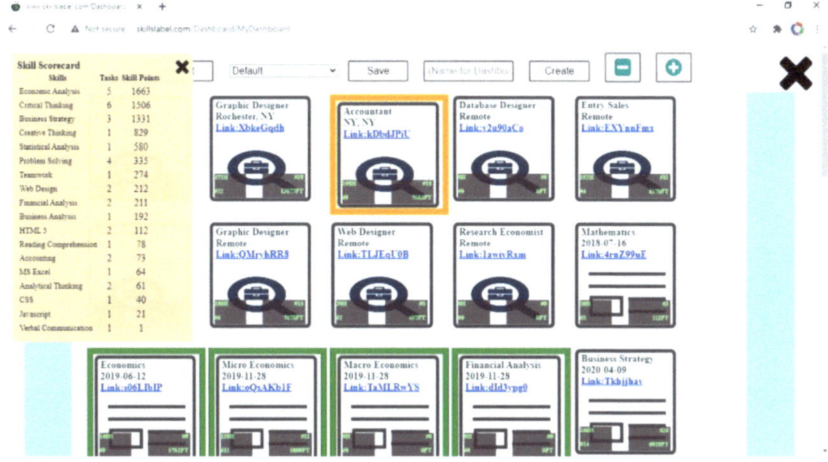

Five Android and Two Microsoft 10 Apps (v 4.0)

There are five Android applications for the learning labels technology (all downloadable from Google Play): Learning Labels Paged Application, Learning Labels Dashboard, Learning Labels Create, Learning Labels Search, and Learning Labels Collections. The first three apps target administrators, including learning practitioners, curriculum designers, workforce developers, teachers, professors, education publishers, and game creators. The last one targets learners. And both administrators and learners use the searching app.

So many devices run Google Android, creating native Android apps is a good way to give more access to learning practitioners on the go. The apps are designed and tested for smartphones, tablets, and Chromebooks. A lot of attention was put on the layout and usage for smartphones; this is the primary reason to keep five separate apps (though there is functionality to move between the apps).

Learning Labels Create

This application allows for a logged in admin user to create any one of the elements. The interface is designed for a mobile, touch enabled device (so limited typing and layering). This is probably the fastest way to create the elements. Once created, they appear as elements in the data set. Later, they could be modified from the website application.

Learning Labels Dashboard

This provides a version of the pure dashboard from the web application. Includes all the same features. Works fast in the native Android grid. Works well not only on smartphones, but also tablets and Chromebooks.

The value proposition is to modify learning pathways and dashboards when the inspiration hits. A teacher before, during, or after a class might think to assign a task to a student or group of students based on the experience. A trainer might modify a training module. Or a job poster modifies job requirements. Simply drag items to make assignments or setup a sort order.

Learning Labels Paged

This is an informative paged application to show the different elements, dashboards, and pathways. The tiles are large and legible and show the skill definitions and aggregates. Navigating through the sections and elements by swiping. Show pathways by marking them in color based on their source.

The value proposition is to change learning pathways. Add elements to pathways without closing a window and navigating through a series. Also, seeing the skills and skill aggregates in a table summarizing the pathways.

Learning Labels Search

This app is a search engine to find learning resources and jobs represented as learning and job labels respectively. There is both a context and skills-based search. The latter is a different take on searching for learning and jobs. Typically, a person searches on a subject matter or discipline.

Searching on skills and skill levels returns different results. With a well-stocked database of learning and job labels, it would be remarkable to see the results of these searches on a macro level across a period. This might prove the relevancy and interchangeability in learning skills across subjects and disciplines, a flip from what we see and expect in our current education, higher education, and training programs. Moreover, it could prove how effective the learning labels system is ten to twenty years from now.

One feature of the app is to choose skill matching where an algorithm changes how the order of skills appears on the labels based on the search result. The search also includes functionality for logged in users. A practitioner might clone, or peer review a label in the search result. A learner might add a label into their collection.

Learning Labels Collections

This is a tasking app for learners to manage tasks assigned to them or they added on their own. From the application, learners access their Skill Emblems – a summary of queued and completed tasks.

There are two Windows 10 Apps: one targets practitioners and the other learners. Both are designed to take advantage of faster processing power on a desktop or laptop computer. The app is also accessible on Xbox game consoles and Surface tablets.

Learning Labels Application

This Windows 10 application combines the four Android apps targeting a practitioner; the advantage is sharing the same login and loading across apps. Considering Windows 10 users most likely use a desktop or laptop (with a larger screen and processing power) this makes sense. The dashboard and navigation between apps is quick.

Learning Labels Learner Application

This Windows 10 application combines the Android apps targeting a learner and the search app. Putting them together allows a learner to work with a search result and get the added functionality of adding them to collections and viewing maps and flashcards.

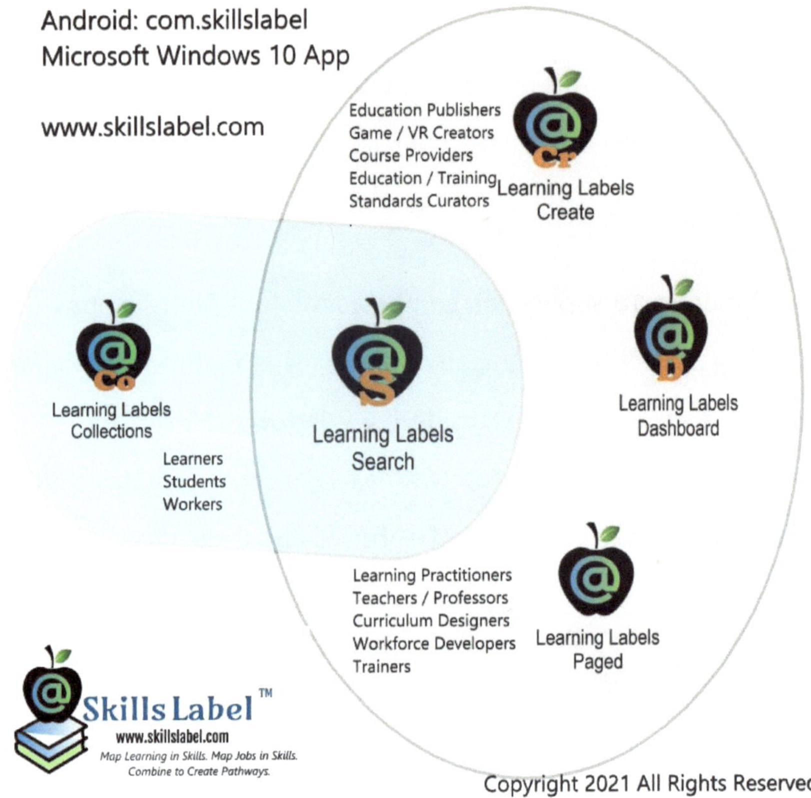

Skills Emblem Real Time Graphic of Skill Achievements (v 4.0)

Summarizing the data from the learning labels for a learner on a skill-by-skill basis was seeded early in the designing of the learning labels system. An earlier version of Skills Emblem is briefly referenced in earlier parts of the book, but the style and uses have been expanded upon in the new apps and on the web application.

A downloadable graphic (PNG) summarizes three data points - number of tasks, hours spent, and number of skill points - for queued and completed tasks. This is helpful to a learning practitioner to understand and contribute to future learning plans and an evaluator to review skill achievements for a job. For complete transparency, there is also a list with links to each of the tasks summarized in the emblem.

A reviewer clicks on the link to see a full page supporting the learning label. As described already in previous chapters, the layered verification process for a learning definition includes referencing standards on the label and a peer review process affirming the standards match the experience. Furthermore, there is a link to the actual resource on the website. If a reviewer questions the accuracy of a label, then they review the resource themselves; this might be worthwhile in deciding from the top pool of candidates for a job, for example.

There are not yet enough learning labels in the system to get a true application of the skills emblem. But a strong future use is to upload the graphic to a social media profile, personal website, or online resume to signal skill achievements. Two advantages from traditional badging are these tabulations are real-time, so update automatically to reflect current learning and directly link to the same skills referenced on a resume or LinkedIn profile.

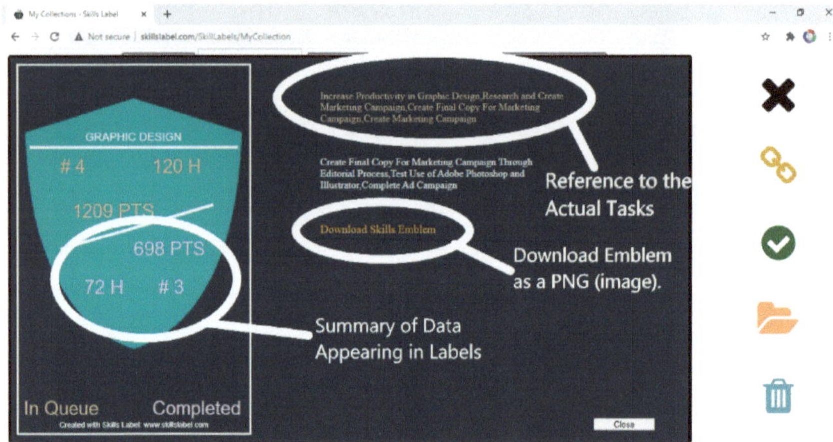

Skills Emblem - Summary of Tasks Queded and Completed on a Skill By Skill Basis

Future Research

Skill Points® 2.0 – Skill Coefficients (v 2.0)

There is already an algorithm to calculate numerical learning gains based on skills (Skill Points®). To take this to the next generation (2.0), improve the algorithm to include a coefficient (growth rate) for each skill (on a skill by skill basis). These are some of the seed ideas. (The assumption is we are using the learning labels technology as a standard representation of learning expectations for tasks or experiences – where Skill Points® are derived.)

Time longitude study (analogous to taking the CLA+ before and after college as completed in a study in the book *Academically Adrift*). Track learning in skills (methods and applications and standards) with a collection of users through time. The groups should represent different stages of learners (education, higher education, and professional development). Take periodic assessments. Aggregate the results. *Construct coefficients based on the results.*

Use current curriculum and credit hour system. Define current learning plans and curriculum in skills (methods and applications and standards). Use current credit hour system and other ways to measure progress. *Construct coefficients based on time, skill, and achieving skills levels*.

Use human learning starting from scratch. Use -pre, -during, and -post assessments to measure how a learner improves in learning skills in a task or experience. Aggregate the results: *match skill to time, level of difficult, and type (quality) of the learning experience*.

Use machine learning / AI starting from scratch. Use -pre, -during, and -post assessments to measure how a system improves in learning skills in a simulated task or experience. Take the results: *match skill to time, level of difficult, and type (quality) of the learning experience*.

These methods are not mutually exclusive. The advantage of the first two methods is they can be started right away. For the longitude study, start once the study is designed. For the curriculum mapping, start mapping a curriculum or learning program. The last two methods require a database of learning labels and the 'human learning' requires a healthy number of users in the system.

My recommendation is to start the first two methods. Build a longitude study for the basic thinking and soft skills; identify students and implement the study (expecting to see results covering a few years). Start mapping curriculum to skills using the learning labels technology. Use the results to get competencies based on the traditional higher education credit hour system (something we want to move away from, but gradually). Another value in this mapping skills to learning is it also applies to mapping skills to jobs and professions.

The idea of numerical learning gains (Skill Points®) is a convincing feature of the learning labels technology. Building them through education, higher education, and a career connects these stages together. The results of this study, new skill coefficient could be immediately applied in the learning labels application.

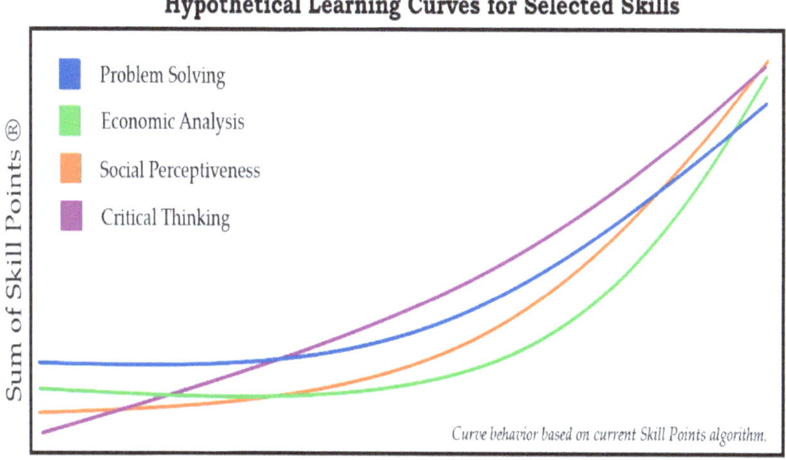

Moving from a Static Display (Screens) to an Interactive System (v 2.0)

In the future, learning is moving to interactive books, games, simulations, and VR experiences. There will be more sets of standards and standards reference other standards (creating a cascading, layering effect). This is what we are already starting to experience now; learning labels application supports four sets of national education standards, three of them were introduced within the last 10 years. Finally, learners will have more options to choose and make decisions in what and how they learn. In a recent report by Pearson, from people around the world, 81% think learning is becoming more self-service.

For all these reasons, a system to manage and track skills (as proposed in the 2016 patent applications) is effective for the future needs of learning development.

Proposal

1. Get learning labels advertising the learning taking place in games and other digital media. Value Proposition: Provide basis of comparison for learners to choose among resources. A tiled, drag and drop interface makes this like the 'Net-flix ifcation' of learning resources.
2. Get learning labels in the games themselves. Value Proposition: Create awareness of learning objectives.
3. Provide access to assessments to verify achievements. Value Proposition: Verify learning is taking place. Give credit for learning taking place outside of the classroom.
4. Allow for learning achievements to be tracked in a system outside the confines of the game's system. Value Proposition: Create a platform to track lifelong learning (in skills).

An example for 1-2 is the age consent label, which appears in packaging and online advertising and usually in the initial screens of the game itself.

An example for 4 is a messaging application, where listeners work across devices and platforms for interactivity with other applications. Also, an operating system might be another example.

Scenarios

Game creators create learning labels for their games to express learning expectations. Might also include assessments to measure outcomes and achievements and produce badges. The system already includes all this functionality.

Scenario 1 – Get game and gamification creators building learning labels.

This provides a way to market and build awareness of the learning taking place in their games.

Scenario 2 (Initial) – Produce static display on initial screen. Optionally provide assessment at completion.

Learning Labels : Crafting a Learning Experience

Setting Up An Experience...

Learning Labels
Set Expectations

Reflect
What Worked

Badge
Earned Credential

Assessments (Quiz)
Pre- , During- and Post Verification of Expectations

There Is Learning...

Each Step Is Supported Within The Application
www.skillslabel.com | www.learninglabel.com | www.educationlabel.com

Scenario 3 (Complex) – Create interactions between learning labels system and the game. At specified segments, produce learning labels and/or assessments. (Functionality like a messaging or operating system).

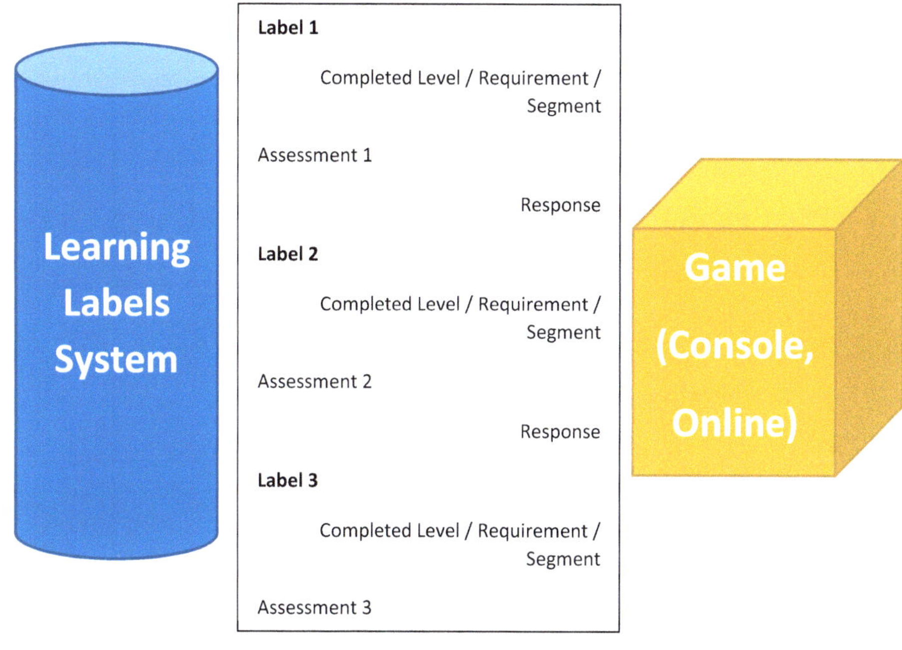

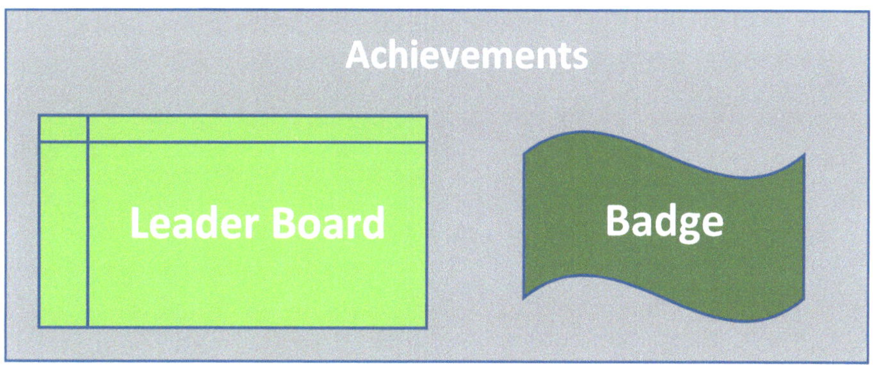

Build Context-Based Search Engine (v 2.1)

There should be an effective search engine for accessing and interpreting learning labels. The seed search algorithm and an interface to manage the results of a search is already built. A context-based search of learning labels is ideal for the following reasons, a learning label is:

- A standard, uniform representation. Defines a single unit of learning and establishes familiarity.
- A self-contained file. Structured as XML file, easy to decouple from website and parse.
- Fully attributed. No need for a database or API request.
- Rich in data. Significant amount of data is represented, in many layers.
- Skills focused. An effective medium to define learning and job requirements.

There are many ways to improve the search algorithm. To be effective, many of the functions require a good number of learning labels in the system; though, much of the infrastructure (database, coded algorithm, and interface) can be built. These are three suggestions:

Create an algorithm to interpret how skills cluster together. A learning label contains between 1 to 10 different skills and their related properties, which include level of difficulty, focus value, standards and methods, and Skill Points®. The research proposal is to construct an algorithm to calculate real-time correlations between skills and their properties on current learning labels and then apply the results into the search algorithm for suggestive ranking. Two value propositions are to help learners find more options to learn required skills and efficiently pivot to other education or career tracks that require some, but not all the same skills.

Understand the growth of skills to suggest a learner's next task, project or course. This coincides with a separate research project to construct the Skill Points® 2.0 algorithm. The research proposal is to use variables Skill Points® 2.0, the learner's current profile and completed tasks, and advanced search input to produce a ranked list of successive suggestions. Two value propositions are to help teachers, professors or trainers design personalized lessons plans for their students or workers and give learners guidance to doing their own, self-guided learning.

Create a version of the search engine to read labels in the context of an XML file. The current search algorithm reads a label, not matching fields in a database. The research proposal is to create a context-based search, which can be used outside the current web application. Allow an interaction to find and interpret labels without requiring a database or API interaction. The value proposition is to provide full access to the labels, making it easier for third parties to adopt the learning labels as a standard representation.

Four Integrations with Artificial Intelligence (v 2.2)

Awhile back (2016), I thought of how artificial intelligence ("AI") could be used in the learning labels technology (but admit I could not explain how AI works). Two main themes of a recent PBS documentary on the influence of AI are: every technology company must consider AI; and it could displace up to forty-five percent of blue- and white-collar jobs. (I mention the latter because much of what learning labels represents is preparing a workforce with skills.) So, I took a course by IBM to better understand the mechanics of AI to communicate how AI could work with the learning labels system my team is working on.

Integration one: verifying the accuracy of skill representations and determining focus values from a learning label. Provide a system with a learning label (structured data) defining the expectations for a learning resource (a book, video, or game) and the resource itself (unstructured data). Create an algorithm that checks each time skills on the label are applied (frequency) and its intensity from the system consuming the resource. For books or videos, this might involve a natural language processor to understand the context of a single body of work. How do we understand applied skills and their intensity from context and questions asked during or at the end of a task or assignment in a book? Or similarly in the transcript of a video? Can we measure thinking, teamwork, and technical skills in segments of a game?

Integration two: creating a learning label by reading or consuming a resource. Building on the first integration, get the system to learn the algorithm to determine skills and their focus values. Provide a system with the resource and get the system to produce a learning label. Can a system learn an algorithm to interpret skills and these properties in this way?

Integration three: understand how skills 'cluster together' to create alternative learning pathways. A learning label is largely designed in skills and related properties (focus and difficulty levels). When there are enough labels in place, take what is represented to understand how skills cluster together. Create an algorithm to suggest effective learning pathways and next tasks in a series. Can we create pathways to pivot between education and jobs?

Integration four: measure skill growth rates on a skill by skill basis. Skill Points® 2.0 is a next generation learning measurement. Again, with learning labels, provide a system with verified learning labels and other variables to determine a growth rate. Essentially, measure how a machine learns skills by consuming learning resources through time. Use the coefficients within the Skill Points® algorithm.

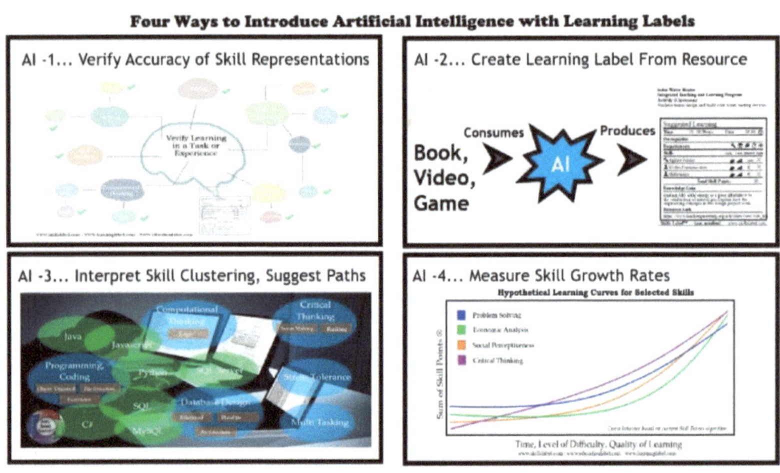

Create More Advanced Skills Parser (v 3.4)

An initial skills parser was introduced into the application to speed up the process in creating learning and job labels, but there is much more potential. The basic idea is to read a block of content/context to generate a ranked list of skills. Some of the semantics include: simply counting the number of times a skill is referenced; correlations to jobs, subjects and disciplines; and finding references to personality traits and interests. These are suggestions to improve the algorithm:

- Link to a text context reader (in AI) to improve reading text and extrapolating.
- Get more precise results by improving reading content and limiting noise (particularly from URLs).
- Evolve the ranking system. Get better through usage and correlation from previous results.
- Expand the database with skills, personality, traits, jobs, and degree. Continue building linkages.

Using Blockchain to Keep Track of Skill Points (v 4.0)

Started to think how blockchain could be a useful way to track a person's progress in acquiring skills. The proposal: a ledger tracking each person's skills; the verification process is a peer review or crowd sourcing; and Skill Points are the currency. What are Skills Points and how is this different than a traditional education and higher education framework?

> Learning objectives have evolved. It's no longer just about knowledge and access. Skills are the new currency." – World Economic Forum

While creating learning pathways and dashboards, there is an apparatus for defining and quantifying learning expectations and job requirements using skills and Skill Points. The basis of the system is to create learning labels on a task / experience level. Make the quantifying process as accurate as possible on a skill-by-skill basis, using a science-based algorithm that gets better through time (Skill Points 2.0).

Summarize Skill Points on the learning labels for a project / lesson plan, course, and job level to design learning pathways. This is a bottom-up approach, which is different than the traditional top-down approach; there are advantages to both.

A top-down approach is defining learning on a credential, course, or job level. The advantage is focusing most of the attention on an accurate assessment, not worrying on tracking learning on a detailed task level. It is easier to match results to macro level demands (like workforce development).

A bottom-up approach is defining learning on tasks and then aggregating them together for higher level elements. The advantage is stacking tasks or experiences in different ways to get desired results. Practitioners pivot between tasks easier. Moreover, the definition process is more static than a substantive credentialing process.

Use of blockchain or another type of centralized tracking system might be an effective way to track a person's development of skills through education, higher education, and professional training. This alleviates the disjointed progression through these stages and makes it easier to effectively create pathways. Clearly, a different approach than the credentialing blockchain movement in higher education. Perhaps a centralized database tracking skills could be linked to the same credentials currently being adopted with blockchain. But tracking skills and Skill Points directly might be more useful in the long term.

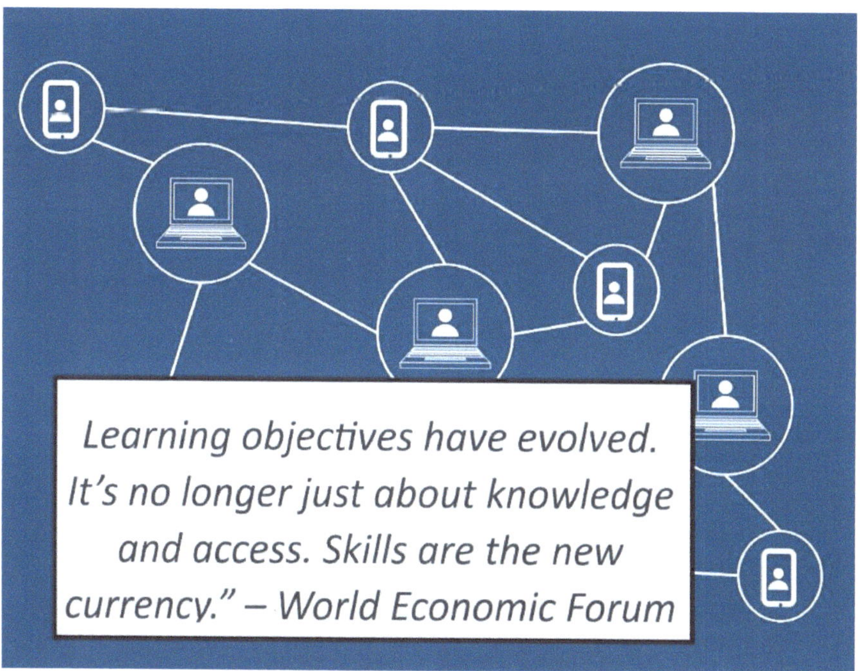

Appendix 1 – Key Terms

Learning labels developed from a display for learning in tasks into a multi-faceted platform. It has advanced, separate interfaces for the two types of users: learning practitioners (administrators) and the learners (students and young professionals). Through development, some names have stuck for the different features and functionality:

Skill Label / Learning label is a patent pending standardized display for any learning task – activities, games, experiences, etc. There are similar types of displays for products and services, such as a nutritional label for food or a resume for professional experiences.

A standardized display in learning has many advantages: tracking learning across education and career stages; a basis of comparison between traditional and emerging learning resources; and portability across media (print, social, and internet).

Label Envelope is a responsive digital container including three items: *an introductory icon, a label, and a credential* earned upon completion.

Label Landing Page is a single page with the label, and all the features to effectively process it – share in social media, give feedback, navigate to the next one in a series, change file types, etc. - as shown in the image above.

Label Wizard 2.0 is the interface a practitioner uses to create a label – takes no more than five minutes. It is a single page with screens to navigate through the elements. The recently released version 2.0 is a stable UI with powerful features (like bringing in a dynamic set of standards for absolutely any skill).

Label Dashboard is a tiled, drag and drop interface to manage the labels. The tiles are represented as the previously mentioned **Label Envelope**. On the right is an icon menu with features to make use of the label. The Label Dashboard has a similar framework for those creating the labels and using the labels but has different functionality.

My Labels (dashboard for practitioners) allows for users to easily manage labels. Users can develop a series of labels based on performance (pass, progress, or fail or ten percentiles) and later view them as a hierarchical structure.

My Collection (dashboard for students and professionals) allows for users to assign labels into collections. Users can also view labels based on skills and access a **Skills Emblem**.

Skills Emblem is a real-time, learning badge for a skill. **Skill Points®** (based on a proprietary algorithm) are calculated instantaneously for completed and in queue tasks.

Finally, there are quite a few domains pointing to Skills Label. So, possible brand names include Learning Label, Education Label, Ed Label, or Skills Emblem.

Appendix 2- Interactivity with Other Skills Applications

Thought of the Skills Based Approach SM ("SBA") methodology in 2011 as I was creating a platform for personal websites. Early on, I recognized skills as a critical element of a personal website. In an abstract way, I see much of the content behind a personal website as presenting and validating skills (two stages of SBA). There are other elements. (For them, there is a framework – Online Personal Brand: Skill Set, Aura, and Identity.) I still feel strongly that most individuals should have a personal website for credentials and signaling skills.

SBA is a methodology centered on constantly cycling through four stages with an evolving skill set. Over the years, SBA has garnered a worldwide audience. I have developed SBA as a basic website application. (And I have been waiting patiently to get this up and running as a mobile application. Ideally, students manage learning tasks on their mobile phones using the SBA methodology.)

Skills Label ™ is a standardized display of learning expectations for any task. The inspiration behind this patent pending technology was to reduce typing in the SBA application. A learning label is a sophisticated, interactive, scalable vector graphic. There is an advanced, stable web application (with a supporting Web API) to create and manage learning labels.

Skill Syllabi ℠ is an application to create and distribute a syllabus for a course. It includes not only the standard sections of a syllabus, but also ones for skills. There is a built-in interface to manage and view a collection of learning labels.

Skills Culture is a growth mindset to learn and apply skills properly – something to motivate and inspire the use of these skills applications. Most people feel they can learn a skill if they put in the necessary time and effort; they learn a skill as much as needed or wanted and there is no requirement to master a skill. A Skills Culture is about being an Agile Worker, someone who is willing to acquire skills on an as needed basis – an effective frame of mind for constant reskilling and upskilling and lifelong learning.

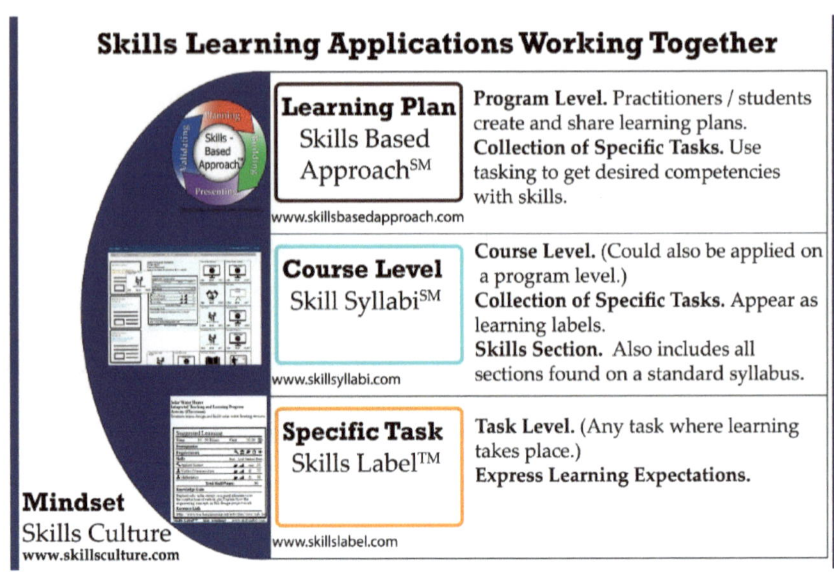
Skills Learning Applications Working Together
Learning Plan
Skills Based
Approach℠
www.skillsbasedapproach.com
Program Level. Practitioners / students create and share learning plans.
Collection of Specific Tasks. Use tasking to get desired competencies with skills.
Course Level
Skill Syllabi℠
www.skillsyllabi.com
Course Level. (Could also be applied on a program level.)
Collection of Specific Tasks. Appear as learning labels.
Skills Section. Also includes all sections found on a standard syllabus.
Specific Task
Skills Label™
www.skillslabel.com
Task Level. (Any task where learning takes place.)
Express Learning Expectations.
Mindset
Skills Culture
www.skillsculture.com
Skills -
Based
Approach

Appendix 3- Links to Video

YouTube Playlists:

Job Labels, Formalize Skills on Labels

Skills Label - Define Learning and Track and Manage Skills

Skills Culture - Growth Mindset for Learning

Skills Based Approach - Methodology for Lifelong Learning

Appendix 4 – Current Functionality Map

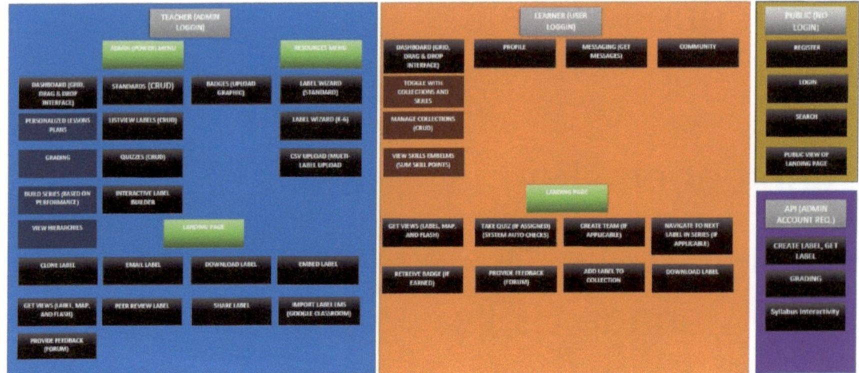

Functionality Map for the Learning Labels Web Application

Appendix 5- Patent Graphics

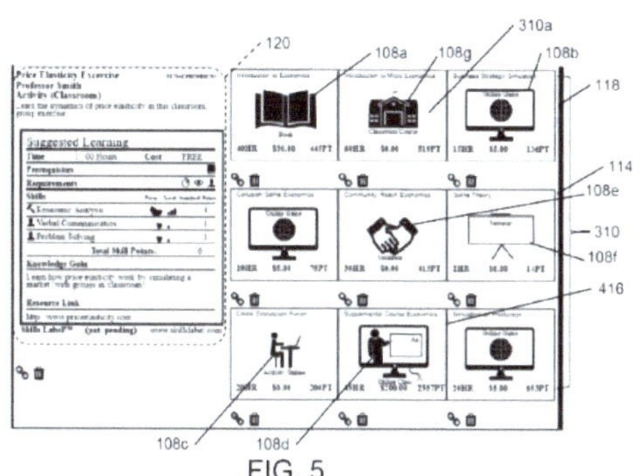

FIG. 5

SYSTEM AND METHOD FOR THE TRACKING AND MANAGEMENT OF SKILLS

[0001] This application claims priority under 35 U.S.C. §119(e) from U.S. Provisional Patent Application [redacted] for "PROCESS / METHOD TO CREATE A STANDARDIZED DISPLAY, CATALOG, AND DATABASE FOR WHAT IS LEARNED FROM CONSUMING AN EDUCATION RESOURCE..." by Ryan M. Frischmann, [redacted] and from U.S. Provisional Patent Application [redacted] for "STANDARDIZED DISPLAY OF LEARNING AND KNOWLEDGE GAINED FROM A RESOURCE OR EXPERIENCE ..." by Ryan M. Frischmann, [redacted] both of which are hereby incorporated by reference in their entirety.

[0002] Disclosed herein is a system and method for creating a standardized format for the display of skills information, and more particularly a format suitable to represent what is learned from any discrete task, resource, experience, project, or activity. The method further involves: defining what is learned, designating a credential gained after "consuming" the resource, verifying learning expectations and outcomes are accurate, and creating awareness and access to the resource within or to a market.

BACKGROUND AND SUMMARY

[0003] There is no current standardized process or common display format for a provider to represent or illustrate what has been learned from a user's "consumption" of an educational resource, or for a user to easily make a comparison of educational resources against one another. In other words, users or consumers of educational

Appendix 6 – Future Proof Vision (v 4.0)

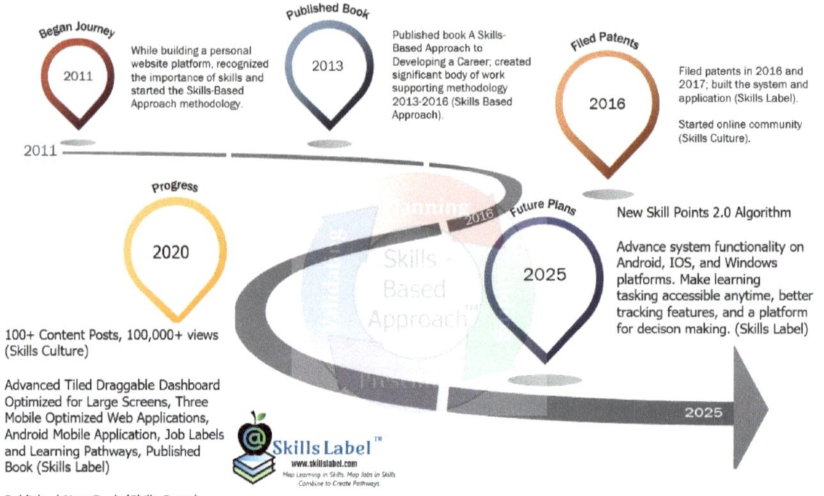

Appendix 7 – Job Label (v 3.3)

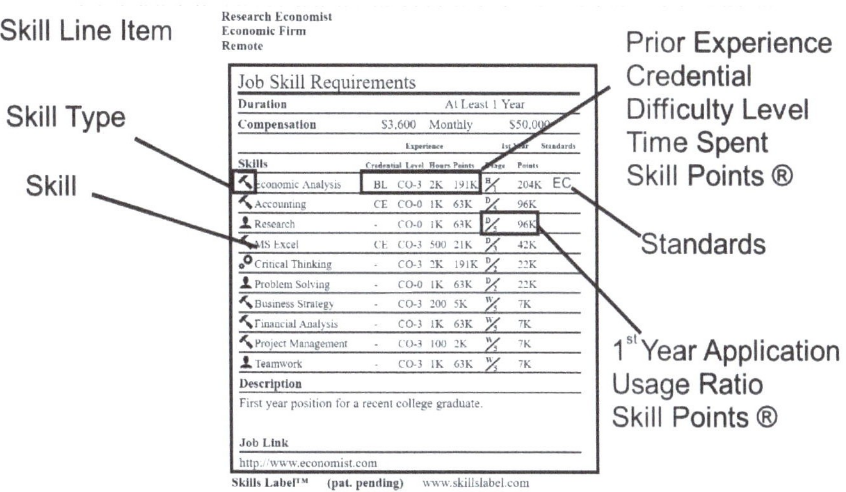

Research Economist
Economic Firm
Remote

Job Skill Requirements

Duration At Least 1 Year

Compensation $3,600 Monthly $50,000

Skills	Experience				1st Year		Standards
	Credential	Level	Hours	Points	Usage	Points	
Economic Analysis	BL	CO-3	2K	191K	B/1	204K	EC
Accounting	CE	CO-0	1K	63K	D/4	96K	
Research	-	CO-0	1K	63K	D/5	96K	
MS Excel	CE	CO-3	500	21K	D/3	42K	
Critical Thinking	-	CO-3	2K	191K	D/2	22K	
Problem Solving	-	CO-0	1K	63K	D/2	22K	
Business Strategy	-	CO-3	200	5K	W/5	7K	
Financial Analysis	-	CO-3	1K	63K	W/5	7K	
Project Management	-	CO-3	100	2K	W/5	7K	
Teamwork	-	CO-3	1K	63K	W/5	7K	

Description

First year position for a recent college graduate.

Job Link

http://www.economist.com

Skills Label™ (pat. pending) www.skillslabel.com

www.ingramcontent.com/pod-product-compliance
Lightning Source LLC
LaVergne TN
LVHW052304100826
845147LV00006B/674

* 9 7 8 0 5 7 8 7 2 9 2 5 1 *